LABOR FORCE

WINNING STRATEGIES DURING PREGNANCY,
MATERNITY LEAVE AND RETURN TO WORK

VIVIENNE WEI

KEBLE PRESS

ISBN:
Hardback 978-1-7326517-2-2
Paperback 978-1-7326517-1-5
eBook 978-1-7326517-0-8

Library of Congress Control Number: 2018909363

For my baby girls, Genevieve and Josephine:
You have unlocked my potential as a fearless trailblazer.
May you live happy, fulfilling lives.

Acknowledgements

I wrote this book to send love and strength to expecting moms at work. But throughout the process of writing this book, I have been receiving love and strength from friends and strangers who made this project possible.

Thank you to the experienced mothers who graciously shared their wisdom and war stories. This book's title, Labor Force, is intended to both acknowledge and celebrate their strength during labor and delivery as well as recognize the importance of their participation in the labor force in the 21st century.

There are many people who supported me as I developed the idea of writing my very first book. I couldn't have done this book without my beloved partner, Jacob. A big reason I can have children and a thriving career is because of him. He is the one always by my side, supporting me and championing me. He took on additional household responsibilities so I could free up some time to write this book. I am grateful to be in love with a man who brings endless giggles from our daughters while I hide in the study finishing edits.

A huge thank you to my mother-in-law, Corine, who is not only family but also my trusted sounding board. She vetted my initial outline, asked intriguing questions and went through several rounds of edits for me. I would not have been able to finish this book without her physical and moral support. Also many thanks to my father-in-law, Brad. Together, they model what an equal, loving partnership looks like.

I am grateful to Chandler Bolt and Marcy Pusey, who showed me the blueprint of publishing a book. A huge thank you to my editors, Aaron Beebe and Katie Chambers, who provided invaluable edits and suggestions in shaping this book and taking it to the next level. My gratitude goes to my beta readers for working wonders: to the savvy strategist Grace Lin; to the ever positive and talented Arum Kang; to the articulate Charlotte Doud; and to the compassionate Marlena Wong.

My gratitude also goes to my Salesforce colleagues for supporting me to launch this book. Annie Vincent connected me with Dan Farber, who provided invaluable advice and support to bring this book live. A huge thank you to Vartika Vaish for starting *Expecting at Work* with me. She makes things happen and has a big heart. I can't thank Andrea Leszek enough for being a trailblazer and a role model. Thanks to my former managers Yuliana Widjaja and Dan Mattrazzo for believing in me and championing me from the start.

I want to thank my close friends for the moral support and encouragement in the launching of this book. A special thanks to Akiko Tateishi, Alika Phipps, Anke Huiskes, Ayesha Fuller, Baily Kempner, Carenina Motion, Celine Dong, Emi Yoshikawa, Elisa Palazzo, Ellen Wu, Gaurav Gupta, Grace Lin, Helen Mou, Ian Weber, Ines Kusturica, Jay Comerford, Jessica Chen, June Yu, Katherine Kadar, Kelli Wolf Moles, Kelsey Morgan, Laura Fox, Mahima Muralidharan, Margie Pearce, Marlene Labastida, Marlena Wong, Minal Mehta, Mindy Hsu, Nicolas de Zamaroczy, Pam Liu, Patricia Ang, Ron Jaiven, Rose Zhong, Sampada Telang, Sara Graziano, Stella Chen, Stephanie Nieto, Thuy Tien Hoang, Tingting Bright and Wendy Williams.

I have always had an insatiable appetite for my fellow mamas' stories. In the case of this book, there were more than two hundred women who completed the survey and shared their stories candidly with me. Thank you to Arum Kang, Ashley Dudgeon, Ayesha Fuller, Baily Blair Kempner, Bridget Frey, Carenina Motion, Charlotte Doud, Christa Quarles, Christine Walsh, Cindy Park, Elizabeth Kwo, Emi Yoshikawa, Emily Zhang, Erin Rizok, Jane Greenthal, Jill Fink, Kelli Wolf Moles, Linda Greub, Lisa Edwards, Mahima Muralidharan, Michelle Bailey, Molly Branch, Nicola Geary, Pam Liu, Sampada Telang, Shannon Bourget, Stella Chen and a host of other women who did not want their names revealed. They were incredibly generous in sharing their stories and giving us a glimpse into their worlds.

I want to thank my parents for nurturing me and providing me with the opportunity to come to the US for its world-class education. Thank you for supporting my dreams, for pushing me to do better, and for loving me unconditionally. Special thanks to my mother, who is my maternal role model. Her entrepreneurial journey gave me a window into what is possible, shaping me to be a strong career woman.

My last and most heartfelt thank you goes to my daughters, Genevieve and Josephine, for whom my love knows no bounds. They inspire me to be a fearless trailblazer and pave the path forward for women in leadership.

Contents

Introduction

Your transition to motherhood will be one of the biggest changes in your life. During this time, you will face many unique challenges, both personally and professionally. Because you are having kids for the first time, these challenges will manifest themselves as entirely new scenarios and you will have to make important decisions in the face of a huge host of unknowns. Of course, it can also be a time of incredible joy, growth, and reflection about who you are and who you want to be.

This is especially true for working women, who are not only navigating the exigencies of motherhood, but are also grappling with their changing relationship with the workplace. Yet rarely are we taught how to navigate those changes successfully so we can make the right career decisions for ourselves.

There is a lot of literature out there about becoming a new mother. But at this point, it is important to consider yourself as a *working professional* as well as a new mother because the two are inextricably intertwined. Your career is an essential part of your identity, and your child's future is determined as much by how you care for yourself as how you care for them.

This book will lead you through an examination of the biggest surprises working women have discovered during their transition to working motherhood. It will close the gap between what you think will happen and what actually happens during pregnancy and maternity leave. And since it can be a steep learning curve, I will also introduce a framework to help you navigate the career decisions you will have to make at this juncture.

As a mother of two and a corporate strategist, I have interviewed and surveyed hundreds of career moms and researched numerous books and articles on the subject of motherhood and work. As a result of this research, I will present you with a set of strategies ready for implementation today, to prepare you for this journey through the corporate jungle with baby in utero.

I will close the book by offering reflections on how best to enjoy this new, exciting life you are creating. After reading this, you will feel much more confident and ready for the unexpected challenges that will arise during this special period.

Working women around the world who are expecting or even just thinking about pregnancy have already experienced a great level of success by adopting the proven techniques and strategies laid out in this book. At my workplace in Silicon Valley, we have implemented some of these strategies. In a survey we conducted in-house, 100 percent of the participants say that they would recommend these strategies to their colleagues who are expecting.

Companies are slowly but surely expanding their parental leave policies to ease women's transition to motherhood while helping us continue to build our careers. By working to further this expansion, we are collectively creating a stronger economy and better futures for the generation we are now giving birth to. The US economy is $2.0 trillion bigger today than it would have been had women not increased their participationsince 1970, according to the US Congress Joint Economic Committee.[1]

This book's title, *Labor Force*, is intended both to acknowledge and celebrate your strength during labor and delivery as well as recognize the importance of women's participation in the labor force in the 21st century. You *can* do this!

By following the recommendations in this book, you will be building a support system to get you through the challenges of motherhood as you pursue a meaningful career, guilt-free. I promise that you will have more confidence in dealing with the unexpected during your pregnancy and maternity leave. And I promise that you will be making informed decisions, helping you realize your full potential.

Don't be the person who says, "I wish I had known this before becoming a mother." Be the kind of mom who loves and enjoys her personal and professional life. Be the kind of mom who people marvel at. Be the kind of mom who others see and say, "I don't know how she does it!"

All you have to do is to keep reading, and each chapter will unveil a set of insights that many experienced moms have learned only after childbirth. They will share their best practices here so that you can make the most out of this exciting journey.

You may find that not all of the recommendations apply to you, but that is part of the fun of motherhood. You learn all the tools and tricks that work for other moms and you get to experiment and decide what works best for your own family. Breastfeed or don't. Work or stay at home. Whatever you choose, you are the best mother your baby could ask for, period. You *will* figure out your own way to make things work. You have a community of us to cheer you on right by your side with no judgment.

This is the ultimate guide to your fulfilling life, complete with wonderful relationships, meaningful work and lots of fun!

Take action toward a thriving family and career today. Stay informed, feel empowered and enjoy this new life journey!

Section I.

Pregnancy & Planning

Chapter 1.

The Big News—When and How to Share This with Work

O n a sunny Sunday afternoon, I came home from my Barre class and my husband, Jacob, handed me a little brown bag.

"I have a present for you, honey," he smiled.

I opened the bag, and in it was a stick, a pregnancy test stick to be more precise.

My period was now several weeks late, and I had also been experiencing discomfort around my chest. Off I went to the bathroom with my present. Sixty seconds later, there it was: two clearly marked red lines on the stick.

"I don't know how to read this, Jacob," I said. As I handed it over to him, I thought, "Am I really pregnant? Is this right? What if this is not accurate? Let's not get our hopes overly high." I wanted to believe, but I needed a second opinion. Just three days ago I had taken a pregnancy test using a stick that we purchased while traveling in India and it had indicated not pregnant.

"You're pregnant!" Jacob brightened up after he carefully examined the stick. There was no question that those clear double lines were the same shown on the instructions.

At that moment, I had mixed feelings. On the one hand, I was excited. This was what I had been hoping for. I had always wanted to have a child and this little person was here, finally! On the other hand, I was a little overwhelmed. In fact, not just a little bit. I was very overwhelmed.

I had no idea what would happen to me physically, mentally and emotionally during pregnancy. What should I expect? This mixed feeling of uncertainty and joy was foreign to me. When Jacob and I had decided to try to have a baby, we had entered completely uncharted territory in our lives. On one hand, I'd been thinking strategically about my career for years and was very aware of just how serious the implications of any missteps might be. On the other, I was feeling a joy at that moment that was greater than I could have imagined.

"I have a lot to learn," I thought.

Later that day, I started to create my work plan for the week. Over the years, I have grown into the habit of spending a couple hours on Sunday evenings checking my work emails and organizing my plan. As I was making my plan, I realized I didn't know what I was going to do with the news at work the next day.

"Should I share this exciting news with people at work? What would happen when I tell them? Could I lose my job? What's going to happen to my career?" The feelings of excitement, fear and uncertainty filled my heart.

I spend almost half of my waking hours with people at work, and yet I didn't know the right way to handle the news with them.

What Does It Really Mean to Be Pregnant at Work?

For the last fifty years, women have been entering the workplace in increasing numbers. Women are earning college degrees and leveraging their education to make greater and more significant contributions to society. In 2017, 34.6 percent of women graduated college or obtained a higher degree, eight times higher than in 1940.[2]

The increase in working women has led to an increase in the percentage of first-time mothers who work during pregnancy, from 44.4 percent in 1961–1965 to 65.6 percent in 2006–2008.[3] Furthermore, women are working closer to their due dates. Research shows that 81.6 percent of those women work up until four weeks before they deliver, a 20 percent increase from fifty years ago.[4]

Despite the higher numbers, it is not uncommon for women to have the same mixed feelings that I had while being pregnant in the workplace for the first time. It is an exciting moment for us personally, and yet professionally many unspoken assumptions still cause concerns for us. I recently held a panel discussion with C-suite executives in Silicon Valley.[5] During the panel prep three out of four panelists shared that they were hiding their pregnancies well beyond the first trimester.

Women choose to hide their pregnancy for many reasons.

First, it is not immediately clear what legal protections exist to protect pregnant workers. Can you still keep your job? What would happen if you need special accommodations?

What happens to your role when you go on maternity leave? What would the employer do to cover your job responsibilities?

Fortunately, since the Pregnancy Discrimination Act (PDA) was passed in 1978, it has been illegal to discriminate against pregnant women in the workplace.[6] An employer cannot fire pregnant workers or refuse to hire a woman because she is pregnant or may become pregnant in the future. In some cases, pregnancy-related complications may even entitle a woman to special accommodations.

Even with PDA in place, there have been lawsuits against employers for such violations. In 2007 the retail operation, Motherhood Maternity, paid $375,000 to settle a pregnancy discrimination suit after the company allegedly refused to hire three qualified female applicants because they were pregnant.[7] Did someone say irony here? Regardless of the dark irony, it is important to understand your rights in PDA and remind your employer of them.

Second, women wonder what their transition to motherhood will do to their career trajectory, not because they will not work hard, but because of bias. They worry that men may be biased and may falsely assume that motherhood tempers a woman's career ambitions. Because of this false assumption, women fear that high profile projects can be taken away from them after they announce their pregnancy.

Additionally, men make up a larger part of the workforce, especially in certain industries like technology and financial services, and they hold more leadership positions. Since men do not experience childbirth, they are more likely to be blind to this concern about career discrimination.[8] In addition, fewer female role models in leadership positions means that women's fears about not having the same opportunities to accomplish their career goals they had prior to pregnancy can be exacerbated.

During my research for example, I spoke with Kate, an associate partner and the second most senior woman at a leading consulting firm. She was torn about the decision to send birth announcements to her C-suite clients who were mostly male. Despite her top-notch work she feared that these clients would discount her capability and choose to work with her male colleagues on future projects.

In the book *What Works for Women at Work*, authors Joan C. Williams and Rachel Dempsey identified what they called a "maternal wall" as the most blatant bias against women in the workplace. According to them, sociologists found that when subjects were presented identical resumes, one identified as being from a mother and one not, "non-mothers got 2.1 times as many callbacks as equally qualified mothers and were recommended for hire 1.8 times more frequently than mothers."[9]

I witnessed this firsthand at a previous workplace. Our team in Australia were interviewing two candidates for a chief marketing officer position, one a mother, and the other a male. After final rounds of in-person interviews, all but one interview panelist preferred the male candidate. Fortunately, this one panelist pointed out that given that the entire panel was composed of men, they should give both candidates a case study to objectively judge their qualifications. In the end, the female candidate was hired because of better analysis of the case study. If they had not administered the case study test, the more competent woman would have been passed over for the role.

Third, some women work for companies whose work culture itself prevents them from announcing their pregnancy. Christa Quarles, CEO of OpenTable, points out, "Industry is not the only differentiator. Specific company culture also makes a huge difference."

During Whitney's four-and-a-half-year tenure at a financial services company, she saw only one woman who went on maternity leave, and she came back two weeks after giving birth. Although the new mother was given a longer maternity leave, she felt the pressure to come back as she was one of the few women in her group.

It was not until my first daughter was nine months old and I joined Salesforce that I realized how much a company culture affects people. It was the first time that I felt I could actually bring my whole self to work.

At Salesforce one of the four key values is *Equality*, and women hold over 20 percent of leadership positions. Andrea Leszek, EVP and COO of our technology organization, has been with the company since 2000, had her children and continued to make strides in her career. With female leaders who I could look up to, I gained confidence that I, too, could be like her.

With my second child, I shared the news with my manager at Salesforce when I was thirteen weeks pregnant, the time after which the risk of miscarriage drops significantly to five percent.[10]

The good news is that some companies are starting to realize the value of attracting female talent and are leading the charge for retaining women. Glenn Kelman, CEO of Redfin, refers to the diverse workforce as "an arbitrage opportunity." He explains that because this pool of talent is not yet fully explored in the job market, companies that foster an inclusive environment can make the best use of the talent to maximize value creation.

Growing and promoting women is a strategic move for companies and shareholders to improve returns. According to a bi-annual study conducted by Credit Suisse, the higher the percentage of women in top management, the greater the excess returns for shareholders. "From YE13 through mid-16, companies where women accounted for 25 percent of senior leadership outperformed at a compound annual growth rate of 2.8 percent; this increased to 4.7 percent at companies where women comprised 33 percent of senior leadership; and then jumped to 10.3 percent at companies where more than 50 percent of senior leaders are women compared with a 1 percent annual decline for MSCI ACWI index over the same period."[11]

One of the best ways to compete for best-in-class talent is to have great benefits. Companies like Google, Facebook and Salesforce have created months-long parental leave and implemented policies to ease women back into work. By taking care of their employees like they are part of a family, companies significantly increase employee loyalty and engagement.

What shapes the company culture is highly dependent on the leadership at the top. Companies with female leadership have some of the best cultures. Christa Quarles is a perfect example. She worked in a male-dominant environment on Wall Street early in her career and felt the pressure to hide her pregnancy. Having been through it herself, she made it a priority to create a supportive environment at OpenTable so her employees could bring their full selves to work.

Most female leaders have been through the journey themselves and know what it is like to be pregnant at work. As a result, they have developed empathetic leadership from their experiences and have instilled a collaborative and supportive culture at their companies.

With these key traits in mind you can seek opportunities at forward-thinking companies to help you unleash your potential in the workplace while building your family.

Consider When to Share the News at Work

While you choose the timing you are comfortable with, you might want to take various business considerations into account to help minimize the impact on your manager and your company.

In a survey I conducted recently, the time at which women choose to share their pregnancy news with their employers ranged across a broad spectrum, from as early as three weeks to as late as thirty-three weeks. Thirteen weeks is the most common, because this is when the chances of losing the child drops significantly. Some women choose to share the news earlier than thirteen weeks because they need special accommodations. Sharing the news with their managers helps them understand the reasons for their requests.

Communicating with an employer before corporate planning cycles helps managers foresee the change in staffing. This helps ensure that your manager has enough time to look for someone to fill in for you and to train the person before you are out.

With my second child, I found out I was pregnant in the late spring, which meant she would be due the following February. I made sure to communicate that news to my manager in the fall because that was when our corporate planning cycle for the following year started. During that planning cycle, he had visibility into his team and the projects that the team needed to complete. He was able to request the necessary headcounts to accommodate my leave and still hit our Objectives and Key Results.

If you are in a client-facing role, you should come up with a communication strategy with your manager. Your clients will appreciate you sharing your plan and being extra available to them before you leave. This allows you to manage their expectations and emphasize that they are important to you. You are the face of your company so handling this professionally will not only benefit you when you return but will also make your company look good.

Share the News with Your Manager and Team Professionally

Now that you have chosen an appropriate time to share this news, plan on telling your manager before your team. This shows your professional maturity and your respect for your manager. Even if you have already told a colleague, share the news with your manager as soon as possible.

You could also use this opportunity to have a very honest conversation with your manager. You will want to ensure your manager understands your commitment and knows you still want and are capable of completing challenging work.

"Maternal wall" bias, the bias against women after they have children, is real and may be subconscious. A lot of assumptions can be unspoken. Lisa Edwards, an EVP at Salesforce, shared a story about a manager on her team who suggested giving an important project to a different person instead of the pregnant member who was more experienced. Edwards advised him to ask the pregnant team member directly rather than making assumptions about her ability to take on more. Other managers may not.

Some managers can be overly considerate by trying not to burden pregnant workers with more projects, but that does not help our career in the long run. According to *Harvard Business Review*, pregnant workers appreciate physical and practical help, such as leaving early to see a doctor, but they are much less enthusiastic about being denied challenging work. Researchers found that the latter type of "help" increased the likelihood that women quit their jobs nine months after their babies were born. They attributed this to a theory in psychology called the threat-to-self-esteem. If a woman keeps receiving the project-related help, it may confirm her fears and insinuate that she is underperforming due to motherhood. [12] It can also decrease the satisfaction a woman feels at work and the amount of control she feels over her own career.

By reaffirming your continued passion for work and your career goals in a direct way, you help your manager understand your motivations and your commitment, while clearly reaffirming your identity as a *working* mother.

We have repeatedly seen that a woman's ambition is not tempered by giving birth to a child. Marissa Meyer was pregnant when she decided to become the CEO of Yahoo. Lynn Jurich, CEO of Sunrun, went on her company's initial public offering roadshow when she was eight months pregnant. Sarah Lacy started her digital media company, Pando Daily, while still on maternity leave.

You, too, can build a satisfying career while having a family. It is your responsibility to educate your manager on how *not* to support you.

Make Both a Transition *and* a Re-entry Plan

As you plan for your maternity leave, you should build a clear transition and re-entry plan and share it with your manager, your teammates and HR. A well-documented transition and re-entry plan includes a list of your projects, meetings, and deliverables, and who will be covering them. This will allow your manager to have visibility into your work as well as a way to plan a seamless transition of your responsibilities to your teammates.

Having a transition plan will not only minimize business disruption but also showcase your contributions. Carenina Motion, a partner engagement manager at Netflix, created a six-page-long summary of initiatives and associated strategies which served as an excellent starting point for a constructive conversation with her manager on coverage and reference for those covering for her.

But planning for the transition *away* from work is definitely not enough. "A re-entry plan is just as important as a transition plan," said Cindy Park, Senior Vice President at the real estate development company, Prado Group. "So many times we try to put the transition plan and all of the work in a perfect form before we go on leave, in order to make the process as easy as possible for our teams. This is valuable, but we should not underestimate the importance of a re-entry plan."

A re-entry plan not only serves as a reminder for you as you return to work but also as a reminder to other team members to officially transfer back your previous responsibilities. Amy, a director of operations at a large retailer, made a plan for re-entry before she went on leave. In the five months leading up to Amy's due date, she had feared that her responsibilities would be divvied up and she would not be able to get them back. Having a written plan helped protect her and her responsibilities after her maternity leave.

Organizational changes happen all the time. Responsibilities can be re-assigned when you are not present; it happens more often than we would like to see. You are the architect of your own career, and you must own your transition and re-entry plan.

It was nerve-racking for me to share the pregnancy news at work, but I realized that it became an opportunity to bring my whole self to work, and I built closer relationships with my manager and my teammates. This is a wonderful moment for you, and people around you will be happy for you if you find the right way to share it.

There is no right or wrong time to share the pregnancy news. You choose a time with which you are most comfortable. When choosing the time, be mindful of your manager and your team's needs. You manager will appreciate being the first one to hear the news even if they are not your closest friend at work. Open communication will give both you and your teammates the space to develop a win-win transition plan together.

◊◊◊

Once you share your pregnancy news, you will want to build up your own tribe. If you work in a male-dominated industry, you are likely the only person who is pregnant on the team. I was in your shoes when I was pregnant with my first daughter. I learned to build my own tribe and I built the same system for other pregnant colleagues across my company.

The upcoming chapters will discuss the various components of your tribe and the tremendous value each component will bring to your pregnancy and maternity. Then we will dive into how exactly you can build your own tribe at work so you can use it to expand your knowledge base and your network throughout the company.

Chances are you have some doubts about the value of investing time in creating a tribe. You might already be tired and busy at work. These doubts often prevent people from building the necessary connections to energize themselves and make their work life easier.

In the next chapter, I will address those doubts head on and will share with you the most efficient way to find your tribe. As many successful women have, you will learn to make the most of your tribe and to make it worth your while.

Chapter 2.

Building Your Tribe at Work

W orking while pregnant has become more common over the last fifty years. Over 65 percent of first-time mothers work during pregnancy today, a 21 percent increase from the 1960s.[13] Because there are more expecting workers, it can be easier to build a support system at work, or what I like to call your "tribe."

Many of us experience numerous physical and emotional changes from pregnancy to maternity leave and the return to work. Having your tribe not only enhances your experience in the office, but also gives you an opportunity to expand your network, helping you maintain motherhood as an asset to your career instead of a liability.

Additionally, your tribe may be able to help you:

1. Expand your knowledge base, e.g., company benefits and resources.

2. Get feedback when you make pregnancy-work related decisions.

3. Share best practices with each other, if your colleagues are also pregnant.

4. Feel supported, which builds confidence in the face of obstacles.

5. Build your network outside of the team.

Support and care from your colleagues can really help boost your energy during those tough times. For example, some women experience severe morning sickness, making it challenging to continue working in the office setting. Dr. Mahima Muralidharan said, "Knowing that you are not alone in the process can be extremely healing."

Drawing from her extensive experience supporting women's well-being in the workplace, Dr. Muralidharan has seen women experience shame in face of pregnancy challenges. Sharing with others in a safe setting makes people realize that others are in similar, if not more challenging, situations. She encourages women to open up in small groups, "By sharing, you realize that you are not so special in the 'shame' category."

Building your tribe at work during pregnancy will help prepare you not only during that period, but also in the early years of raising your child. Research shows that "women drop out of the workforce not because of lack of mental capacity, but because of the culture. They frequently feel not supported or respected, for raising a family while pursuing their careers." [14]

Miranda, a data scientist at a pharmaceutical company, said that if it were not for her manager and teammates frequently checking in with her and showing that they cared, she would have quit her job, because "doing it all is really tough during those early years."

Cultivate Your Tribe

Your work tribe consists of four key types of people: your manager, your teammates, mommy mentors, and fellow expecting moms at the same company.

The most obvious person in your tribe at work is your manager. You and your manager work together to develop your projects, key deliverables and your long-terms goals. By communicating clearly what you are capable of and what you are constrained by, you help set expectations with your manager and develop plans for optimal outcome.

The next set of people are your teammates, with whom you likely interact frequently. You probably sit close to them and may even go to lunch with them on a regular basis. Through working on similar projects, you build rapport and trust by supporting one another. They will likely cover for you during maternity leave. Every little bit of help you can offer to them will put goodwill in your relationship "piggy bank," which is essential if you want to make future withdrawals in the form of help later on.

The next two sets of groups are the less obvious ones and can sometimes be harder to find. Mommy mentors are experienced colleagues who have become moms while working at your company. They have gone through something similar and can offer many practical tips and advice. Sometimes, because those women had children earlier, they have returned to work and built their seniority in the organization. These relationships can and should develop into potential future working relationships or sponsorships.

Lastly, your fellow expecting moms at work are experiencing the same excitement and challenges that you are. Those women can empathize with you and understand your exact situation. They serve as great sounding boards, especially given that they are working at the same company with the same culture.

Tap Into Your Company Network

Since Sheryl Sandberg published *Lean In*, we have seen Lean In circles pop up around the world both within companies and by locations. In fact, research found that over 90 percent of Fortune 500 firms have some type of affinity, networking, or resource groups.[15] These are valuable networks for you to tap into to help you identify your tribe.

Salesforce is the leading enterprise technology company founded by Marc Benioff in San Francisco in 1999. At Salesforce, everyone is treated like a family member and we refer to ourselves as an *Ohana*, a Hawaiian word meaning family. One of our core Ohana values is equality. To live this value, we have a set of affinity groups that are Salesforce-sponsored and employee-run. These groups are run by employee volunteers in their spare time, and all the events are sponsored by the company.

For example, we have the Salesforce Women's Network (SWN) for all women and allies. On a monthly basis, our volunteers organize events to enrich people's work experience, from fireside chats with senior leadership, to panel discussions on integrating work, family and wellness.

Furthermore, SWN also serves as the umbrella organization for subgroups supporting more targeted interests, including *Salesforce Moms' Network*, *Women in Technology* and *Expecting at Work* groups. *Expecting at Work* was a subgroup that my colleague Vartika Vaish and I started together to serve expecting moms at Salesforce. Once we announced this initiative, over eighty women working for the company around the world signed up within twelve hours. (You will learn more about how to start your *Expecting at Work* initiative later in this chapter.)

Now, you may say I am lucky to be in an organization like this. Indeed, not every company has a strong family-friendly culture and all the existing support infrastructure in place. This is typically influenced by company leadership, and in my case we were extremely fortunate to have an open-minded CEO focused on long-term strategies.

But equality was not an espoused value for our Ohana on day one. It took many trailblazers voicing their opinions and influencing our leadership to make that happen. Marc attributes our value of equality to our Chief People Officer Cindy Robbins and Executive Vice President Leila Seka, because they proposed the importance of women in leadership.[16] Since then, we have launched women's conferences at Dreamforce and have made tremendous strides in recruiting, retaining and promoting women.

Photo: Marc Benioff and I, when I was 29 weeks pregnant.

You may be in an organization without these established support systems, but you are not alone in this journey. Like Cindy and Leila, you can also be the initiator. You can build a network to tap into if it is not already there.

When I set up *Expecting at Work*, I reached out to one of SWN's executive sponsors and founding members, Andrea Leszek, a Salesforce veteran. She has grown with the company and also helped shape the company we are today. Andrea shared with me that when she was pregnant at work in the early days of Salesforce, there were less than 1,000 employees and the majority of them were men. Maternity leave policy had not been defined, so she had to work with HR and management to build the policy. When she first returned to work from maternity leave, she and a few other pioneering moms, like Suzanne DiBianca (executive director of Salesforce.org at the time), suggested creating a mothers' room and were able to do so with the support of Parker Harris, co-founder and CTO.

It was people like Andrea who blazed the trails and paid it forward for all of us.

You, too, can be the change.

Expecting at Work Circles

The Harvard Business School (HBS) alumnae network introduced me to the concept of circles.

My friend Jill Fink, who graduated from HBS in 2005, saw that women, including her classmates, had significant life changes after they transitioned to motherhood. During her HBS reunion weekend in 2015, she organized a session for all of the alumnae to get together and share their experiences.

The event received overwhelming responses from alumnae all over the world.

Upon realizing the value of sharing and learning from our experiences, she decided to take it further by working with the HBS alumni office to launch HBS alumnae circles.

A circle typically includes a group of six to eight women who graduated from different classes and backgrounds. Six to eight is a good size because it allows people to open up and be vulnerable with each other. And by bringing in women with diverse backgrounds, we have more enriched discussions and enhanced learnings.

Circles meet on a monthly basis to discuss topics ranging from personal to professional and family. Because we spent two years attending the same business school, we shared experiences that connected us immediately. I have been with my circle for one and a half years now and have fostered long-term friendships with these women.

With the positive experience from my HBS circles, I thought it would be wonderful to have this at work for pregnant colleagues. When I was pregnant with my first child, I felt alone during the entire pregnancy. I was working in a male-dominant group at a male-dominated company, and the few women we had were in their early twenties.

Luckily, through a random introduction, I met another woman who was pregnant in a different part of the organization. The bond and knowledge we built together carried me through the rest of my pregnancy. I am so grateful for the random introduction. Looking back, I wish I had built more such connections.

You are going to go through a lot of similar changes and challenges as some of your colleagues, and you could benefit from learning from and supporting one another. Working at the same company is the shared experience, which provides more connections and can be a great way to learn about areas of the company you are not familiar with.

How to Start a Circle

The second time around, I was determined to make a difference in my pregnancy experience and in those of my fellow colleagues.

First, I did some inquiry into what support systems existed. I reached out to Salesforce Women in Technology (WIT) to inquire if there were already any groups like this. I think you already know the answer. It did not exist, but I was encouraged to explore the needs of my colleagues and start one if necessary.

During this inquiry phase, I also met Vartika Vaish, an engineering lead who sits on the WIT committee. She does not have any children, but is inspired by the cause and the initiative. She became my founding partner, which was an unexpected, pleasant surprise. Just when you think you are alone in this journey, you will be surprised by the love and support you get from people around you.

Second, we needed to understand if such a demand existed and the size of the demand. We determined that our internal company Chatter would be a good medium through which to explore this need. Chatter is an enterprise social network and a Salesforce product. (Yes we drink our own champagne!) It allows employees to share knowledge and drives productivity.

We started our Chatter Group, *Expecting at Work*, and posted on the forum. Within twelve hours, over eighty women signed up to join the group. If you do not have a company social network, you can start your group by working with the women's organization or HR to see if you can get sign-ups that way.

Third, from the newly formed group, we surveyed to see if there would be interest in joining an *Expecting at Work* circle. The meeting would happen during lunch time, so we would not take away time from already busy expecting professionals. Based on availability, pregnancy stage, and location, we set up two circles in one week.

The key to the success of the circles is commitment. We are all very busy, so this needs to be something people were willing to consistently commit to. Your experience depends largely on other people's contributions and sharing and every single participant matters. Often, we tend to forget how much we matter as individuals. We do matter, and we matter a lot to not only ourselves but the women around us.

Here are the three steps to building your own *Expecting at Work* circle:

1. Find others to help you start the circle.

2. Figure out the demand and post the group on your network's forum or through HR.

3. Get opinions from the members on when and where to meet and ensure everyone understands the commitment level.

We surveyed the participants in the *Expecting at Work* circles pre- and post-participation. One hundred percent of the participants said they felt more confident and ready for their maternity leave and that they would recommend circles to their colleagues who are expecting. "The best part of the circle is to be able to talk about everything and anything pregnancy-and-work related in a safe environment," said one of the participants.

Photo: My colleague from my circle, Charlotte Doud, and I volunteered at the Homeless Prenatal Program and met with the Founder Martha Ryan and Development Director Kristin Hatch.

I know the process of finding your own circle sounds like a lot of work, but it only takes a few outreach emails and conversations. Your reward for doing so will definitely outsize your efforts. I benefited tremendously from the amount of knowledge sharing and support I received. In the circle, I learned everything from understanding company benefits to handling a sticky work situation to turning a breech baby.

As it turned out, I found out that I had a breech baby five weeks prior to my due date. Babies in breech positions are heads up, rather than heads down. Doctors usually recommend a C-section to ensure the baby's safety. After learning about possibly having to have surgery, I spent many sleepless nights with an already exhausted and pregnant body. I simply could not stop thinking about the scar that the C-section was going to leave on me, forever.

So during our monthly meeting, I anxiously shared my situation with my circle. Surprisingly, the love and advice they gave calmed me down. My colleagues made various suggestions on how to turn the baby. I tried many of them, and despite the lack of success, the love and goodwill behind those suggestions made it okay for me. I felt a true sense of camaraderie with this small group of women, with whom I continued to learn from and share my experience with during and after maternity leave. While I'm only briefly mentioning this here in the context of building your tribe, it really deserves its own chapter (See Chapter 5).

Because circles can and should be diverse, we also have an *Expecting at Work* group on Facebook that includes people from many different companies, where you can learn from experienced moms and support other expecting moms. You are invited to join us today by requesting access on Facebook.

You are not on this journey alone in the workplace. Get out there today and start building your tribe. Those women are waiting for you to meet them. They will help make your transition easier and smoother during your pregnancy and return to work.

◇◇◇

While it is important to have your work tribe help in this transition, you are also embarking on a journey that involves a newfound commitment to your non-work life. Because your goal is to enhance and align *both* aspects of who you are, you will also want to align your expectations and responsibilities with your partner during pregnancy.

In the next chapter, you will learn how many moms-to-be discovered surprises about their partner after having their baby. You will also learn a set of strategies to help you prepare your partner and family for this journey ahead. By setting realistic expectations, you and your partner will be happier and stronger, which will make everything easier.

Chapter 3.

Your Partner Is
Half the Work

"Make your partner a real partner."

- Sheryl Sandberg

A s Sheryl Sandberg points out, if you want to continue having a thriving career, you will benefit from establishing a true partnership with your significant other.

As mothers, we start doing a lot more work well before the baby is born. We carry our child in our body for forty weeks with all the nutritional and lifestyle responsibilities that entails, while our partner does not have the same responsibilities.

Our job doesn't get easier when the child makes their debut into the world. This new, vulnerable life depends on us. That means most of the basic things we do for ourselves have to be repeated for someone else, every single day, until they are old enough to take care of themselves. Without an active partner to help with everything from feeding and diaper changing to cleaning or something as seemingly simple as burping, the work is endless.

In the meantime, we may still have a full-time job as well as other responsibilities around the house. A study by sociology researchers Pamela Stone and Meg Lovejoy found that two-thirds of the women who decided to quit the workforce identified their husbands as a key factor. When their partner refused to make compromises or increase their participation in caregiving, the woman had to fill a so-called parenting vacuum.[17]

When you and your partner lean in together, the new childcare responsibilities become much more manageable.

Conceptually I understood Sandberg's point, and my husband and I mutually agreed to share childcare responsibilities. It was not until I had my first daughter that I recognized the importance of putting the right system in place to establish a true partnership.

Ever-Changing Expectations

Theoretically, having someone to share the work with should make things a lot easier. What surprised me was how hard it was on my relationship with my husband, especially in the early days.

My husband, Jacob, and I met randomly at a church party in 2014. We were the only two people who did not attend church, but were invited by our respective friends. I still remember the moment I stepped in the door. He walked up to me and said, "Hi! I'm a California boy but I don't surf." He quickly realized that his line did not work on me and changed tactics. Instead, he shared that he was a PhD turned data scientist. That immediately piqued my interest because I was looking to hire a data scientist on my team. We hit it off right away. Although I did not hire him at work, I did bring him on to my personal team. We were engaged in six months.

Perhaps because we got engaged and married soon after we met, it felt like our honeymoon never ended. We were two professionals living in downtown San Francisco. We had a great balance of couple time and alone time. We went out together or with our friends. We pursued our own hobbies and career dreams. I traveled to Amsterdam and Mexico often for work, while Jacob had band practice and teaching engagements at the General Assembly outside work. We were living the dream.

We had always known we wanted to have kids and were both excited to welcome our first daughter, Genevieve. Having kids was a decision we made together. However, upon her arrival, it seemed like I was waking up to a nightmare.

"Why is Jacob not doing X, Y, and Z?" I constantly thought to myself as I got up at three in the morning every night during the first three months to pump in order to increase my milk supply. Having a child was clearly much harder on me than him.

Disgruntled, I started to understand what actually happens after a couple has children. Comparing couples with and without children, researchers found that the rate of the decline in relationship satisfaction is nearly twice as steep for couples who have children than for childless couples.[18]

As moms, our expectations of our partners change significantly (at the exact moment that we lose any time we used to have to communicate those expectations). We are no longer individuals who only take care of ourselves, but rather, we become individuals with emotional ties to a new life. Especially after carrying this new life for forty weeks, we, as mothers, want to give everything we can to him or her.

I put a tremendous amount of pressure on myself to be a good mother. For example, I read about the positive, long-term impact of reading on children's cognitive development in HBS Professor Clay Christensen's *How Will You Measure Your Life*. I immediately resolved to speak to Genevieve for at least 30 minutes every day from the moment she was born. Without discussing it with him, I expected Jacob to use all of his free time to read to Genevieve.

Because of expectations like this, I had endless new demands for my husband. Regardless of what he did and how much he did, it just never seemed enough.

In my case, when my husband did not live up to my expectations, it became a burden to me. His interests and hobbies were becoming annoying shortcomings. I often thought negative thoughts about him: "Who drinks beer and watches baseball games on Sundays? Shouldn't he be playing with our daughter and reading to her? Why does this little creature have to eat every three hours and why is he not feeding her?"

One day he looked at me. "What would make you happy, honey?" he asked.

I stumbled. I started to think about what would make me happy. At that moment, I realized that taking care of a newborn was much harder than I had ever expected. I had put a lot of pressure on myself and expected him to meet my ever-changing expectations as if they were his own. I also never took the time to externalize my self-imposed stress and challenges by articulating how he could help.

It was as if lightning struck.

How was my husband supposed to know what my challenges and expectations were when I never discussed them with him? "Being a good father" is simply too general. Everyone has a different definition of a good father. It is as if your boss were telling you to be a good employee and then lashing out at you later, without ever sharing her expectations and discussing what your biggest contributions could be.

According to psychotherapist Tina Tessina, PhD and author of *Money, Sex and Kids: Stop Fighting about the Three Things That Can Ruin Your Marriage*, "Your relationship will not be a priority during this time. The more realistic you are about that beforehand, the less resentful you'll be when it happens."

Having children will likely be a shock to your marriage. Your expectations may change due to the many unforeseen circumstances that arise in these early days. It is important to take the time for yourself to think through your goals and discuss them with your partner, after which you can jointly brainstorm to find a solution.

Establish a True Partnership

During my interviews with career moms, many shared that they had made plans to share childcare responsibilities with their partner well in advance of their baby's arrival. When your baby arrives, there will be little time for sleeping, let alone planning. Because many responsibilities, such as breastfeeding, fall on you, you should consider delegating some other responsibilities to your partner so that you can have some rest.

Elaine, a product leader at an e-commerce company, shared, "I had planned for my husband to change all the diapers during his paternity leave." When their daughter arrived, her husband Mitchell executed on the plan. This gave Elaine some time to rest and bonded him with their daughter early on.

Research shows when fathers are hands-on with their newborns during the earliest moments, these experiences create a bond that keeps them more involved with their children later on.[19] To this day Mitchell reads to their daughter on a regular basis and spends a lot of quality time with her. The undivided attention from him helps boost their daughter's self-esteem and confidence in the long run.

Establishing a true partnership with your husband starts from the moment you are pregnant. Here are a few easy approaches that can help establish that relationship between you right away:

Prenatal Check-Ups: On average, a woman has to go to twelve to fifteen prenatal visits, which is time consuming for you. But those doctor visits are not just regular visits. Rather, they are an important way for the fathers to be engaged throughout this journey. It's worth the time for both of you to go.

Even though your partner is not the one getting the check-ups, it is important for him to make the effort to make time for the visits. Doing so will help your partner feel he is contributing and connecting with the baby and supporting you. It also allows him to be present in case there are important decisions for you to make as a couple.

Paternity Leave or PTO: During the first couple of weeks, you may want your partner to plan on using any paternity leave he may have, or his accumulated PTO. You shouldn't plan on doing this alone. Having a partner to burp and soothe the baby after each feeding lets you sleep more, and by going through the sleepless nights together, you will build a bond in raising this child. Your partner will experience changing numerous diapers, getting up in the middle of the night, and washing milk bottles, which gives him a chance to understand your joint responsibilities in a way only those early days can provide.

Trust me, when your body is still hurting from childbirth, you will want your partner to be right by your side to help soothe the baby. Even if your division of labor changes later on, he will always appreciate the hard work you are putting in because he experienced it firsthand.

Rigorous Planning of Responsibilities: Today, women are assuming more home responsibilities, even though more of us are in the workforce. The term "second shift," coined by Arlie Hochschild, is commonly used to describe employed mothers facing an unequal load of household labor and thus a "double day" of work.[20] In "Women in the Workplace 2016," produced by LeanIn.Org and McKinsey & Company, researchers found that "Women in senior management are seven times more likely than men at the same level to say they do more than half of the housework." [21]

By religiously planning out the responsibilities with your partner, you can alleviate friction, especially during pregnancy and the early phases of infant care.

After realizing that we had made the mistake of not planning our individual responsibilities during the pregnancy, Jacob and I spent some time doing so after our first daughter arrived. We discussed and planned our individual responsibilities on a whiteboard with each of our names listed side-by-side at the top and the list of tasks underneath the names.

By writing out those tasks for each of us, we were able to visualize the work being distributed somewhat evenly. Doing this together also allowed each of us to contribute by playing to one's preferences and strengths. For example, Jacob was responsible for all the diapers during his paternity leave during the day and at night while I exclusively breastfed. We set aside time to do tasks together: family story time is one of our favorite activities.

This planning exercise helped align our expectations and removed vagueness. We became much happier.

Adaptation to Change: Even if you've planned in advance, it is just as important to revisit the plan against the actual situation, especially when there is a change in infant care arrangements or work schedules.

When Jacob first returned to work, I was staying at home. Uninterrupted sleep became a necessity for him, so we agreed I would take over the night duties exclusively. Fortunately, our daughter was often sleeping five hours per night by then, so his return to work wasn't too disruptive most of the time. But at times it was exhausting.

A couple of weeks later, he came home with flowers and a smile. "Thank you for letting me rest at night. I know it is a lot of work for you, and I appreciate you."

These words melted my heart and made all the hard work worthwhile. I also know that if he had not experienced the sleepless nights himself, he would not have had the same appreciation he does now. His paternity leave made this connection possible.

I am incredibly grateful to his employer for providing paid paternity leave, which is only available to 15 percent of all American employees.[22] More importantly, Jacob might have not taken the leave if it had not been for the encouragement from company leadership.

Unfortunately, many men who are offered paternity leave choose not to take it. In a survey conducted by Deloitte, "fewer than half of the respondents feel their company fosters an environment in which men are comfortable taking parental leave."[23] Having HR policy is not sufficient to achieve workplace equality. Leaders need to lean in and encourage men to take paternity leave.

While we are fortunate to have such generous benefits, it is in a company's best interest to encourage their employees to take the parental leave. When an employer is supportive of family values, it tends to build employee loyalty and trust. In the tech industry where competition for talent is fierce, generous family leave policies drive retention and help companies stay competitive. Furthermore, employees are incentivized to work harder and go the extra mile. I have repeatedly witnessed and supported my husband while he burnt the midnight oil coding or running analyses.

Get Ready for "The Nothing Box"

One of the biggest surprises for many women is the mental exhaustion of motherhood. From the moment we find out about our pregnancy, we start to worry about their well-being and to plan activities to help them grow better. That constant planning and worrying never ends. In fact, when they arrive, we plan and worry even more. If not managed carefully, we can easily lose ourselves and our identities.

Our partners, on the other hand, may still be able to enjoy themselves (those endless football, basketball and baseball games, all year long).

Indeed, men's and women's brains are wired differently. Penn Medicine published a brain-imagining study that shows the stark contrast.[24] Researchers found greater neural connectivity within one hemisphere in men, suggesting their brains are structured to facilitate connectivity between perception and coordinated action. They are often good at one single task at hand. In contrast, the wiring in women's brains goes between the left and right hemispheres, suggesting that we facilitate communication between the analytical and intuition.

As a result, men are generally better at single tasks and compartmentalizing them while we have superior memory by connecting our world from car payments to work to baby to shopping. This connection means that we are constantly thinking and constantly worrying.

Mark Gungor, a renowned marriage expert, coined the term "the nothing box." He describes men as having individual boxes: one for the job, one for the kids, one for sports, and one for the mother...somewhere in the basement." (I could not help but laugh at how accurate it is!) There is one box where they think about *nothing*.

There is not much we can do to get rid of their "nothing box." However, we can offload and share some of our mental exhaustion by assigning them specific tasks. This is extremely valuable because adding a baby to your life can mean doubling your housework sometimes if you do not actively delegate responsibilities.

Arum Kang, CEO of a start-up CoffeeMeetsBagel, shared her insight that even though she and her husband are both pursuing their career dreams, they do their best to have an equal share of responsibilities. She keeps a running list of tasks for him to do at the beginning of each week. That way, everyone has the same expectations and can work toward the common goals.

While you will likely be constantly managing the household, the bright side is that you get to hone in on your leadership skills.

◊◊◊

Egalitarian career expectations have to come with egalitarian family arrangements. Having a child can often widen the gap between your expectation and reality if you have to constantly fill the childcare void. You can drive equality at home through planning and managing responsibilities with your partner early on.

It might be difficult for your spouse to split responsibilities with you exactly 50/50 due to work constraints. Every family is different. The key is to plan with your partner early and actively, so he can participate as much as possible. My friend Christina, a mother of two and a career mom, is married to a firefighter who is away on duty for one month at a time. While her husband takes on more responsibilities when he is home from his duty, she is on her own when he is away. The sacrifices they make as a family for our community are enormous.

During it all, you might get help from your family. In the next chapter, I will share the advantages and pitfalls that

come with such help. You will learn about the technique to
cope with those pitfalls.

40

Chapter 4.

The Cherry on Top—
Support from Family

G rowing up in China, I was an only child born in the early
1980s when Mao implemented the one-child policy. My
parents treated me like "a pearl in the palm" and devoted all
of their energy and resources to me.

At eighteen, I left Shanghai for the first time and landed
in Hanover, New Hampshire, to attend Dartmouth. It was
the first time that I had been away from home for more
than two weeks, not to mention that I was in a completely
foreign country with people speaking a language that was
not practiced much back home.

Since then, I have traveled the world and worked and lived
in different countries. Every time I visited a new country, I
would send home a postcard from the city. When I was visiting
Victoria Falls in Zambia, I remember walking two miles to get
to a local post office downtown in order to send the postcard.
That was me in my twenties, living far, far away from home,
chasing my dream and living life to the fullest.

After I met Jacob, my parents started to be more involved
in my life. We visited Shanghai as a couple for the first time,
and Jacob asked my father for his permission to marry me.
My parents practically planned the entire wedding in front
of the Oriental Pearl TV Tower in Shanghai.

When they found out that I was pregnant, they started planning their trip to California to help with their new grandchild. It was the first time in twelve years that my parents and I had lived under the same roof together.

It is a tradition that Chinese parents help their children raise the grandchildren. When I was born, my grandmother on my mother's side lived with my parents for the first year. She cooked postpartum meals for my mom and shared all the traditional practices on recovery from childbirth. When my mother had to go back to work after taking one year of maternity leave, my grandparents on my dad's side came to live with us. Grandma cooked dinner for us while grandpa helped pick me up from school in a pinch. My mom was able to work late if she needed to.

By taking care of me, my grandparents leaned in to support my mom's career so she could continue to chase her career dreams.

My family's story is not uncommon. According to the Shanghai Municipal Population and Family Planning Commission, 90 percent of the city's young children are being looked after by at least one grandparent, and half of these grandparents provide exclusive care, a number that is increasing.[25] Many of my Chinese friends have their parents and their Chinese in-laws take turns to visit them in America and help provide childcare.

It was an unspoken plan that my parents would come and help out. They would prepare our meals and clean and help with the baby whenever I needed. This was part of the culture. They were part of the tradition and would be paying it forward.

However, tradition came with what seemed to be baggage. My parents strictly stuck to the so-called "Chinese confinement" as part of my postpartum recovery plan. I was told not to shower or brush my teeth during the first month. Laying in my bed, feeding the baby and eating the specially designed postpartum meals were my only responsibilities. In addition to all those strict rules, I had to live through unlimited amounts of "nagging" and "I told you so."

After not having lived with my parents for more than a decade, I went from living like a free bird to being a trapped bird. It felt like I was back in my childhood again, but worse.

Understand That Every Family Is Different

My experience will not be your experience. Every culture has its own way of interacting between generations and there are benefits to each.

After my first daughter was born, I talked to some of my friends with babies. What surprised me was how unique my family support was compared to many of their experiences. In the US, most couples are practically on their own when they have kids. Many live far away from their families. Some families visit the new parents and their grandchildren for a few weeks. Whatever support they get is considered the cherry on top and cannot be expected.

At the same time, many couples will say that they relied on their friends for that support and that having their parents visit was more stressful than helpful. The important thing is, whatever your situation, look for that support where you can. I can't say it enough: like your relationship with your partner, getting help from your "family" is more important than the conflicts that may arise from it. And well-voiced needs can make the stress more manageable.

After my conversations with my friends, it became clear to me that what I was taking for granted deserved a lot more appreciation. Many new mothers would trade anything to have the kind of help I received, especially in those early days. Gratitude helped me relax and reduced my stress during times of conflicts.

Moreover, my parents were just expressing their love. There was a generational gap between us, preventing me from seeing this at first. They wanted me to have what worked for my mom. I was the one that interpreted their recommendations as "I'm not good enough."

Lastly, help often comes at the expense of great sacrifices made by the helpers. Six weeks after my second daughter was born, my parents had to return home unexpectedly. I was still recovering and could hardly walk. My mother-in-law made a commitment to drive three hours every Monday to help for four months straight, rain or shine. She is an amazing and patient influence on my daughters, and we learn volumes from her each and every visit.

You may or may not have support from your family and friends. If you do, whatever you can get is a huge bonus. It feels good to appreciate those people around you because they truly care about you and your happiness. There are going to be moments of conflicts. Those conflicts, including who is right, matter less in the grand scheme of things.

Keep your eyes on the bigger goal: building a happy family.

◊◊◊

With that goal in mind, you can now begin to really focus on what's happening to you and your child during your leave from work. In the upcoming section, you will learn about the surprising challenges that women face while they are on maternity leave. By design this will get a little personal: sharing stories is an important part of embracing the growth opportunities that are on offer during this period. In the next chapter, you will hear a few of the real stories that happen during the early days of becoming a mother, from living with an unexpected C-section, to being tied to your baby 24/7. From these stories, you will learn how to overcome difficult experiences and hear about a few of the resources available to you.

Then, even as you experience this steep learning curve at home, you will also get an insider look into what is happening at work and how to stay on top of your game. I will also share the best resources for you to tap into to address those challenges.

What Really Happens on Maternity Leave

–

Chapter 5.

Early Days of Darkness

"Wah. . . wah . . . wah . . ."

I frantically looked at my watch and there it was: 5:15 a.m. This was the third time in the last three hours that Genevieve had woken up screaming. I swore it was less than ten minutes ago that I had changed her diaper, fed her and rocked her to sleep. Then here she was again: crying.

"What could she want this time?" I whined to Jacob, who had also been up all night helping me with our five-day-old daughter. I was exhausted, frustrated and deeply saddened. Our daughter seemed to be unhappy, and yet I could not figure out why. It was time to repeat the process: change, feed, rock her again, and again, and again. . .

Don't Think You're Going to Sleep Well

I would be doing you a huge disservice if I didn't tell you about the biggest open secret in the transition to motherhood: once the baby is born, all hell breaks loose.

When I was pregnant, I was frequently told that having kids is the most rewarding experience one can have. It certainly is rewarding, but no one told me how hard it was going to be in the early days. Perhaps they were trying to not worry a pregnant woman, but I wish somebody had set my expectations.

Those early days are hard. Really, really hard. To attribute the difficulty to sleep deprivation alone is an understatement.

I started my career in investment banking, where I worked a hundred plus hours per week on a regular basis. Depending on the urgent deadlines, I might have to stay up all night at the office preparing Excel analysis and PowerPoint presentations for board meetings.

Sleep deprivation can be incredibly painful, but the early days of motherhood takes it to the next level. In comparison, staying up all night in front of a computer screen seemed like a walk in the park.

The thing is, having a newborn is not just about waking up every hour. It's also relentless. Unlike pulling an all-nighter or working a long week, demands from new babies don't stop. Ever. Not during the day, and definitely not during the night.

At a panel discussion I hosted,[26] one of the panelists shared a personal story about her sister who had had a baby girl recently. Her sister said to her, "I thought having a child was supposed to be joyful. Why do I feel like I am not doing anything right?"

Arum responded, "Who said this was going to be joyful? The early days are really hard!"

It might be difficult to see the light at the end of the tunnel, but know that this phase will end. It does get better.

Resources on Combating Sleep Deprivation

Sleep deprivation is commonly experienced by new parents during the early postpartum period. According to Dr. William C. Dement, a sleep specialist, parents of newborns lose about two hours of sleep per night until the baby is 5 months old.[27]

Lack of sleep can have a significant impact on relationships and work performance. According to a study by the Rotterdam School of Management, even one night of poor sleep can seriously affect workers' decision-making and reduce their ability to "regulate their impulses." These negative behaviors can cost the US economy $200 billion a year.[28] That is one of the reasons why it is beneficial for employers to provide parental leave, so you can rest during the early postpartum period and perform at their best when they return to work.

If you suffer from sleep deprivation as a new parent, here are a few tips from experienced moms.

1. *Share the Nighttime Responsibility:* There are several ways to do this with your partner. Elaine's husband changed all the diapers and brought their daughter to her for nighttime feeding every three hours. Amy and her husband split the night into two shifts: one from 10pm to 2am and the other from 2am to 6am. If your partner has to work, you can still get his help on weekends and/or the 10-midnight shift. It doesn't have to be 50/50, but the key is to share it.

2. *Delegate Tasks:* If you have family members or friends who are willing to help, you can ask them to take on some chores. They can also help bottle-feed your baby so you can rest a bit longer. Several moms also recommend using meal planning services, so they don't have to spend time on planning or grocery shopping. I alternate between Home Chef and Dinnerly, which has been a huge time saver. We like to be independent and be in charge, and one of the best ways to do that is to mobilize our

support system and get the help we need to recover sooner.

3. *Invest in a SNOO If You Can:* With our first daughter, we religiously followed Dr. Harvey Karp's "5 S's" from *The Happiest Baby on the Block*, often referred to as the "sleep bible" by the moms I interviewed. With the advent of Dr. Karp's SNOO, a smart bassinet that rocks baby to sleep using the same "5 S's" principles, we decided to give it a try with our second daughter. I let the technology do the hard work of getting my daughter sleep, and it worked like magic every time. Despite the high upfront investment, the average cost of $7 per night is much lower than getting a night nurse.[29] The SNOO is one of the main reasons I was able to write this book while taking care of my newborn daughter on maternity leave.

4. *Other Select Resources:*

   • *The Baby Book* by Dr. Sears is an encyclopedic guide to the first two years of your baby's life.

   • *Mayo Clinic Guide to Your Baby's First Year* is easy-to-use yet comprehensive how-to manual that covers it all, from baby-care basics to month-by-month development to common illnesses to health and safety.

   • *Lucie's List* (www.lucieslist.com) sends you a weekly email with practical advice and insights during and after your pregnancy.

"Have a Sensible Birth"

Birth and early child-care are often traumatic and hard. It's not all sunshine and smiles.

Childbirth is one of the most impactful things our bodies endure. Our body has to fit this little growing baby inside itself for forty weeks, adjusting our organs to make room for the baby. The birthing experience is painful, whether it is a vaginal birth or C-section surgery. During those first few days, it hurts to do the most basic things: walking, going to the bathroom, or even sitting up straight, etc.

During my interviews, Victoria, a partner at a law firm, jokingly said, "I was surprised to come home with a diaper, on me!" By the time we get home from the hospital, our bodies are not healed enough to effortlessly handle the things we need to handle. But we still have to handle them.

Over the years, I have heard many surprising birth stories. My friend Sabrina was rushed to the hospital in a taxi and felt her baby's head coming out as they were crossing the Bay Bridge; she barely made it to the hospital, let alone having time to get an epidural. After eighteen hours of painful labor, Arum had to have an emergency C-section because her baby refused to come out and had an infection. My friend Shannon tore her cervix so severely during the birth that she received two blood transfusions immediately after delivery; she had lost so much blood in the delivery room that the hospital had to send several cleaning staff to clean off her blood on the walls.

Story after story, I thought I had built the resilience to expect the unexpected until my own story happened.

My first daughter was a vaginal birth. Everything was smooth sailing: she came right on her due date, I had an epidural as requested, and there was barely any tear during the birth. With my second, I was very relaxed about the entire pregnancy as I thought I was going to have the same experience. This lasted until my thirty-five weeks' check-up when I found out that my baby was in a breech position. My doctor said I would have to have a C-section if the baby did not turn.

"This was not part of the plan!" I teared up on the way home from the check-up. Shocked and stressed, all I could think about was the scar that would be left on my belly, forever.

I reached out to my mommy tribes at work, and support and advice started coming in. A fellow expecting mom, Charlotte Doud, shared the Spinning Babies website (www.spinningbabies.com) with me. I tried everything, from Webster Technique with a chiropractor to external cephalic version to yoga. There were moments of lightness and joy, like when I tried to practice forward leaning position and my two-year-old daughter saw me and joined me by doing the exact same position.

But in the end, nothing worked.

"I am sorry that you have to have a C-section." Jacob tried to comfort me as I was lying on the hospital bed waiting for the procedure to begin, "Remember when we did our five-hour birth class during your first pregnancy? The one piece of advice that I remember very clearly from the doula was 'Have a sensible birth.'"

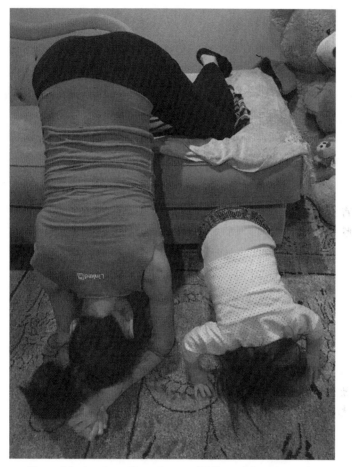

Photo: My daughter, Genevieve, and I. I was thirty-six weeks pregnant with Josephine.

My second daughter was in a complete breech position (where the buttocks are pointing downward with the legs folded at the knees and feet near the buttocks) and the doctor could feel her little foot dangling down my pelvic floor. There was a risk of umbilical cord prolapse causing dangers to her and my own life. The sensible thing to do was to have an emergency C-section at thirty-six and a half weeks.

I was incredibly grateful for Josephine's healthy arrival. Besides the C-section, I did not have any complications and she did not have to go to the NICU. Upon finding out about the emergency C-section, my mother-in-law gave up all her prior commitments to drive down to pick up Genevieve from school, allowing Jacob to accompany me throughout the entire surgery. I was so fortunate to be blessed with all the love and support.

Resources about Delivery and Recovery

While the early days and years of raising a child are incredibly difficult, what never fails to amaze me is the incredible love that we receive from other mothers. These are the women who notice that you are pregnant and give up their seat for you on the subway, the women who help you reach the top of the fridge for milk in the grocery store, and the women who share their experience on how they got their babies to take a bottle for the first time.

There are several free or inexpensive resources that you can tap into on day one.

1. *Mommy and Me Classes:* Held in the hospital where you give birth, you can sign up for free classes after your baby is born. You meet with the same group of women for ten–twelve weeks, and each session is led by a nurse who will discuss certain aspects of raising a baby. The topics range from sleep, feeding, developmental milestones and managing stress. The beauty of those classes is that you are in the room with the same group of moms who are trying to figure out the same things you are

for the first time. "It feels good to know that I am not alone and others are struggling too," my friend Emily shared. "I made friends with these moms and still have play dates with them, as the kids are so close in age."

2. *Local Mothers Club:* In your local area, you most likely have an existing mothers' club organized by mom volunteers. They organize kids' activities, clothing swaps and walks in the park. Mothers' club is a fantastic group because members are mothers with kids of similar ages as you or with older kids, which means they have a lot of experience and knowledge to pass down. You can also use referrals from other moms to find reliable childcare later on.

3. *Facebook Moms' Groups:* Various Facebook groups have been formed by users to support women. Those groups provide a forum for people to exchange ideas, ask questions and get advice from group members. Topics range from pregnancy to first-time moms to working mothers. In those early days, it can be challenging to make it to in-person meetings. Facebook groups allow people to connect virtually and offer an alternative to making connections and to ask for help. You can request to join our *Expecting at Work* group today.

4. *Other Select Resources:*

    • *The Birth Hour* (www.thebirthhour.com) is a podcast of birth stories that helps pregnant women achieve an empowering birth experience through sharing authentic birth stories.

- *The Birth Partner* by Penny Simkin is a guide to childbirth for dads, friends, relatives and other labor companions to help new mothers.

- *The Journey* (www.thejourney.org) provides other women's accounts of dealing with postpartum depression. Hearing these stories can be very powerful when you feel isolated.

Don't Let Breastfeeding Rob You of Your Worth

Just as I was recovering physically and emotionally from the childbirth while figuring out how to take care of a newborn, I also had to deal with what I see as the biggest blind spot going into the postpartum period—the hardships of breastfeeding.

I had already read many books for first-time moms. I knew that feeding baby breast milk could help keep babies healthy. The World Health Organization (WHO) recommends that mothers breastfeed their children for the first two years. In fact, when you Google the word "breastfeeding," the second prompted word is "benefits."

What is frequently left out of those search results is how much stress the idea of breastfeeding can cause and how dispiriting it can be if it doesn't just happen "naturally".

From the first day of childbirth, doctors and nurses will remind you of the importance of breastfeeding and the right techniques. They will probably tell you how your body is "made" to do it, and how instinctual it is for both you and the baby. Then they will help you get the milk flowing by positioning the baby properly so they can latch on correctly.

Once you figure out how breastfeeding works, you are supposed to aim for volume. During my hospital stay I was given a medical grade breast pump, a machine that you hook up to your body to stimulate your breasts for more milk. After every feed, my baby went to sleep and I was expected to pump to make more. It is uncommon for new mothers to *not* suffer from cracked nipples or encounter issues of some sort.

However, many lactation consultants will simply say, "Yes, you are in pain, but keep going."

Don't get me wrong. These professionals are experts who will teach you all the tips and tricks to make your breastfeeding successful. However, there are a lot of expectations, and it can be overwhelming to want to not only live up to your own expectations, but also those of your baby, your family, your baby's pediatrician *and* the World Health Organization.

During the first few weeks, I would pump after each feeding in hope of keeping the leftover and freezing it. Time and time again, I barely produced anything after pumping for thirty minutes. It felt like my efforts were not generating any results. I distinctly remember the concerned look my dad had on his face while he stared at the few drips I had just pumped. "You are not making enough breastmilk."

The feelings of self-doubt, frustrations and fears crept up on me. I went on the internet, bought all kinds of supplements and joined several Facebook groups asking for help. When I saw people posting pictures of their freezers full of stacked breastmilk, I felt incompetent as a mother.

Just as I felt those negative feelings were about to eat me alive, I came across Jessica Shortall's *Work. Pump. Repeat.* She enlightened me with her inspiring manifesto, "Your worth as a mother is not measured in ounces." The last thing I needed to hear was from some random person on Facebook, "Oh, your body is made to do this." How can anyone else know what my own body can or cannot do?

More importantly, I realized that I was so wrapped up in my ability to produce breastmilk that I was not enjoying my time with the object of all this effort: my precious daughter. My goal was to have a happy family. This constant stress over breastfeeding was keeping me from my goal! While breastfeeding can be beneficial to babies, it has very little to do with competence as a mother. While difficult at times, I eventually learned to be more relaxed about breastfeeding.

While the memory of those early days is stressful, the long-term commitment can make breastfeeding even more difficult. I found that it was almost impossible to go anywhere for a long period of time because I either had to feed Genevieve every two to three hours, or pump to relieve my engorged breasts. When I did manage to go outside, I always ended up spending half the time looking for a spot with some privacy to feed her. I was no longer a free bird traveling the world whenever I wanted to.

When Genevieve was about five months old, a group of my friends decided to go to Napa on a food and wine tasting tour to celebrate my friend's baby shower and relax in the countryside. Jacob willingly stayed at home to look after Genevieve. I was so happy to be out of the house and see my girlfriends again.

To prepare for the trip, I estimated that we would spend seven hours, so if I pumped after three and a half hours, I would only need to do it once away from home to minimize interruption and maximize my presence. Napa was a two-hour ride from San Francisco where I lived so by the time we reached the second stop, Matanzas Creek Winery, I would be able to pump in a private room that they reserved for me.

On the day of the trip, I pumped right before leaving and brought my electric pump with me. Just as I thought I had this all carefully planned out, we encountered significant traffic on the road. By the time we arrived at our first stop, Bartholomew Park Winery, I was already fully engorged and felt so much pain in my chest.

"It felt like they were about to burst," I shared with my girlfriends. We hectically looked around for a private space, in vain. I had to go to the women's bathroom next to the tasting room. Unfortunately, the only electrical outlet was by the bathroom door, so one of my friends guarded the door.

Eight months later, this experience came up in a conversation I had with the friend whose shower we had been celebrating. "I didn't fully understand why you had to go to the bathroom to pump so badly at my baby shower, but now I really do!"

If you're committed to breastfeeding while returning to work, building a milk stash on maternity leave can be a very helpful way to get back some freedom while ensuring that your baby can still be nourished with breast milk. Your partner or family can help feed your baby while you are away for a break. It can also help prepare for your return back to work because your baby will have a full day of supply while you are at work. And when you do choose to stop breastfeeding, you can prolong the time that your child drinks breast milk from the stash.

Resources on Breastfeeding

Here are some great tips from interviews with other moms and my personal experience.

1. *Start Pumping As Soon As Possible*: Breastmilk usually does not come in until a couple of days after your baby's arrival, but pumping after each feed will send your body the signal to make more. The more signals your body receives, the more you will produce. Before my first child, I read that there was a risk that I might produce too much if I pumped too early, but in hindsight, I wish I had done it. Rarely do you hear a mom complain about making too much breast milk. I'd like to use the faucet analogy: you always have the option to turn off the faucet if the water is gushing through; there is very little you can do if it is the other way around.

   Please note: You don't have to do this additional pumping after each feed. You will be exhausted in these early days. Do the best you can, and give yourself a break. It's going to be okay.

2. *Invest in a Good Pump and a Pumping Bra:* Your pump and pumping bra are going to be your new friends, so you will want to make sure they meet all your criteria. The hospital-grade Medela pump is the strongest and works great during your hospital stay, and you can also rent one to bring home for a few months if you'd like. After reading numerous product reviews and trying various pumps, I decided on the Spectra S1 and absolutely love it because of its warm pink design, the backlight

and an auto-timer. With its minimal pump noise, I manage to go right back to sleep during my early morning pumping sessions.

3. *Buy an Inexpensive Portable Pump for Travel*: A portable breast pump can offer a great level of flexibility and convenience when you have to pump occasionally away from your baby. These pumps don't take up a lot of space in your bag and are often manual, so you don't have to worry about finding an electrical outlet. Had I gotten one of those during my girls' trip, I would not have had to pump right by the bathroom door.

4. *Get a Deep Freezer If You Have Room*: You can store your milk stash in bags specially designed for breastmilk. Putting your stash in a deep freezer allows you to keep the milk for up to twelve months. A deep freezer could also come in handy when you need to store pre-planned meals or feed the family well in a pinch.

5. *Other Select Resources:*

    •   *La Leche League* (www.llli.org) is an international organization that provides information and support to breastfeeding mothers. You can join free meetings locally, led by experienced volunteer leaders.

    •   *Work. Pump. Repeat.* by Jessica Shortall provides practical tips for breastfeeding after your return to work.

    •   *Kelly Mom* (www.kellymom.com) is an excellent blog that provides evidence-based information on breastfeeding.

Just like anything related to motherhood, breastfeeding is a personal choice. Ultimately, you have to do what you feel is most comfortable, as it does take away so much from a woman: time, freedom and headspace. There is a reason our grandmothers and great grandmothers thought formula was the best thing since sliced bread.

◊◊◊

No child birth experience is the same, but what we all have in common is the will to make it work. This experience is what makes us incredibly resilient and strong.

It might seem like the changing diapers and breastfeeding every couple of hours are endless, and that your body is recovering so slowly, but this is just a temporary phase. I was once told that with babies, "the days are long, but the years are short." It is amazing how quickly we forget the pain we endure to bring a new life into the world. We come out of these tough times as our stronger and better selves.

While you are trying to survive those sleepless days and nights, a lot could be happening at work. It might be overwhelming to think about work right now, as you are still figuring out this new job of being a parent.

But I promise you that it does not actually take that much time to stay in touch with work if you approach it in a structured way. It will be that much easier for you to return to work weeks later. After interviewing over a dozen experienced moms, they all noted that going back to work was extremely difficult and that part of the challenge was the change in the workplace.

In the next chapter, you will learn a few things you can do now to minimize the disruption to your work. By planning ahead, you can smooth your transition back to work and do it all.

Chapter 6.

Out Of Sight, Out Of Mind—
What Is Really Going On At Work

O ver the last few decades, we have made tremendous progress in protecting women's legal rights. While US federal law protects workers from losing their jobs due to pregnancy or maternity leave, the US is far behind other countries. Out of the world's 196 countries, the US is one of only four that has no federally mandated policy to offer paid parental leaves.[30]

Take its neighbor Canada for example: women can take paid maternity leave for up to one year. New parents in Sweden are entitled to 480 days of leave at 80 percent of their normal pay.[31] That is on top of the eighteen weeks reserved for mothers, after which the parents can split up the time however they choose. These policies are considered normal for citizens of developed nations.

With paid maternity leave policy, new mothers can recover from childbirth and bond with their babies without worrying about paying the bills. Healthy mothers can be more productive and stay in the labor force longer. Countries reap economic benefits in the long run as half of the labor force can return to work to contribute to the economy.

Fortunately, some pioneers in corporate America have recognized these benefits and have begun implementing generous maternity leave policies. In late 2015, Netflix came out with one year of fully paid maternity leave, the first of its kind. Quickly afterwards, other companies followed suit by providing paid maternity leave.

By doing so, companies are able to attract the best talent and avoid the high cost of replacing a highly valuable employee. Research shows that it costs 20 percent of an employee's annual salary to replace that person due to training and the time required to bring one up to speed.[32] When Google extended the maternity leave from twelve weeks to eighteen weeks in 2016, the rate of new mothers quitting dropped by 50 percent.[33]

While it is still a luxury to have prolonged maternity leave, it also means that you may be going back to a different job with a different manager. Even if you return to the same job, your job responsibilities may have changed.

Let Go of the Anxiety

When I was pregnant with my first child, I had a really difficult time letting go of my job responsibilities and I didn't take the full leave. In California, we had one month of disability leave prior to the due date, of which I took only two weeks. At the time, the company I worked at offered twenty weeks of maternity leave with 100 percent pay.

Despite the generous leave policies, I decided to return to work after eight weeks in order to lead a strategic planning project with high visibility in the organization. I had a reputation for being a strong performer and wanted to defend my reputation after I had my child. If I could have, I would have pretended that the birthing experience had no impact on me. I wanted to be "one of the guys."

When I was on leave with my second child, I was contemplating returning to work early again. It was not until I read Sarah Lacy's *Uterus is a Feature, Not a Bug* that I realized that this anxiety was common among many women. "[In the US,] we view leave as a privilege, a 'perk,' not an entitlement. As a result, some 60 percent of women in tech feel the pressure to shorten or forgo their parental leave."[34]

Baily Kempner, a private equity principal and Kauffman fellow in New York, went through a similar experience. Despite her firm's six-month maternity leave policy, she thought it was "an unfathomable amount of time." She pointed out that this feeling was due to "a fear for one's own self, a fear for becoming irrelevant."

In my case, I reached out to a group of experienced career moms in Canada and the UK to get their input on my decision, since in both of these countries women are legally entitled to up to fifty-two weeks of maternity leave. When I shared my thoughts, they persuaded me to take the full twenty-six weeks off. These are highly motivated moms who are investment bankers and lawyers.

There are a few reasons I will counsel you to do the same, if possible:

1. *First and foremost, this is a once-in-a-lifetime chance to be solely responsible for your family and your new baby.* Ayesha Fuller, a private wealth banker and a mother in the UK, shared her dilemma on taking her maternity leave. Her manager supported her and empowered her to take the full leave, "You never get that time

with your baby back." Remember: the days are long, but the years are short!

2. *Second, maternity leave is only a small part of our thirty-plus-year career.* It rarely makes any difference to cut it short by a few months. Nicola Geary, a partner at Cassels Brock & Blackwell in Canada, says, "Once you're back, people won't remember whether you took three months or six months. Reintegrating won't be that different. And in a year or two, those few months will have made zero difference in your career, but will have made a big difference to you and baby."

3. *Third, your decision to take the full leave will impact the many who try to build a family and a career in the future.* My friend Pam Liu described a possible scenario if I cut my leave short, "If you are given twenty-six weeks and you don't take it, I can only imagine the company execs sitting there saying 'Well, we offered a generous leave, but the women didn't even seem to want it...'" Indeed, for most women in the world, this is not a conversation you'd have to have. In the US, we still have a long way to go, and it is by our collective power that we can shift the change for the better.

"Blaze a trail and then be a mentor, advocate and ally for the women that follow you," said Erin Rizok from the Ontario Ministry of the Attorney General.

So I chose to be a trailblazer. I learned to compartmentalize and make the most out of my precious maternity leave.

I followed the advice from Baily, who decided to take her full six-month leave. Rather than letting fear take over, she set aside a few hours per week to connect with other experts in her field. She took advantage of her six-month maternity leave to expand her network, which she did not have time to do while working.

I have a great company, team and job to go back to. My company is a pioneer in championing women in leadership. The last thing I want is for executives to take the leave policy back because they do not think women want to take them.

Embrace the Ever-Changing Job

In today's world, companies are evolving at a rapid speed, especially with the rise of technology. As industry dynamics shift, incumbents that have been around for a long time find themselves going through restructuring and reorganizing to defend their businesses. Disruptors are embracing innovation through fail-fast mechanisms where they themselves make lots of organizational changes to drive effectiveness. Quick sprints and iterative processes are becoming the rule rather than the exception.

Reorganization does not always mean downsizing. Rather it is a way for companies to realign their teams with strategic goals to enhance effectiveness. While you are on maternity leave, discussions may be happening behind the scenes.

Rebecca was about to go on her six-month maternity leave. She knew that her organization was going to go through a significant reorganization, but no changes had been announced yet. She was very anxious about her leave, as she feared that she would be missing out on opportunities and would not be able to ramp up quickly enough upon her return. She did not want maternity leave to derail her career trajectory.

What were the best practices for Rebecca while she was on maternity leave? We came up with a five-part plan for her to stay abreast of the ever-changing industry landscape and company priorities.

1. *Do What Makes You Feel Most Comfortable.* This is your maternity leave and you own it. During this special period, the first and foremost priority is to ensure the health and happiness of new moms and babies. As I have mentioned previously, you will be going through really challenging early days of motherhood. Do not feel pressured to work while you are on maternity leave if your body and mental state are not up for it. Maternity leave is for maternity!

2. *Set Expectations with Your Manager.* It is up to you to decide how much you want to keep in touch with your manager and share your preferences. Most managers will respect your maternity leave and leave you alone. In Rebecca's case, she wanted to be kept in the loop on maternity leave, so prior to her leave she asked her manager to message her with major updates. She explained to her manager that it would help alleviate some of her own concerns about the team and allow her to stay in touch with business changes.

   One month prior to Rebecca's return, she set up bi-weekly one-on-ones with her manager to discuss her projects upon her return. She made it known that she wanted to use the gradual return-to-work benefit where she would work four days a week for the first month. Bringing it up in advance allowed her manager to restructure the projects for the team to deliver the best results. Keeping open communications works both ways. It allows you and your manager to come up with a plan to facilitate your very own maternity leave and your mindful return to work together.

3. *Check Emails on a Regular Basis.* Rebecca set aside fifteen minutes to check her emails weekly when she started her maternity leave, but she did not reply to those emails. This allowed her to stay connected with her team and her work without overburdening herself. You can determine the frequency of checking emails based on your needs. Tina G., a Wall Street analyst, checked her emails and followed the market daily while on maternity leave. It would have been extremely difficult for her to come back to work if she had checked out completely. As a result, transitioning back to work was very easy for her. Others may not have to.

4. *Read Industry and Company Updates.* Stay connected with industry landscape and company updates by continuing to read industry reports and following the news. Rebecca followed the news feed on Salesforce Chatter, the enterprise social media, monthly. During her leave, she also applied to attend Grace Hopper, an annual women-in-tech conference scheduled two months after her return to work. Her industry knowledge continued to make her an asset

to the business and opened more doors to future opportunities.

5. *Maintain and Expand Your Network.* Once things calm down and the baby is settling into a rhythm, maternity leave can be a great time to maintain and expand your network. Structuring some time out of your day to meet with other professionals allows you to stay relevant and sharp. After three months, Rebecca felt much better physically and arranged a few informal lunches and coffee chats with her manager and teammates who became her friends. Her team got to meet the baby for the first time, and she got to catch up with them.

Rebecca went on maternity leave, but she chose not to completely disconnect. It was the choice she consciously made for herself. However, she waited to connect with work until she got the hang of being a first-time mom and her daughter was breastfeeding well. She felt significantly less stressed once she built a mutual understanding with her manager that she would get updates from her manager about any changes to her team and her role. Staying connected during her leave also eased her back into work.

◊◊◊

Even if one stays connected to work during maternity leave, the decision to go back is not an easy one. I have met women who have made the decision to permanently stay at home without taking a long-term perspective and now wish they had taken various factors into consideration before making that decision.

In the next chapter, you will learn of a tool that you can use to decide between becoming a stay-at-home mom or a working mother. You can measure the possible outcomes of your options and evaluate them. Quantitative results combined with qualitative can provide a holistic approach to this complex decision-making process.

Chapter 7.

What Is Your Career NPV?

At this point, you have delivered your baby, your baby is growing at a healthy pace, and your body is recovering. You are nearing the end of your maternity leave.

A question that frequently comes up is, do you go back to work or become a stay-at-home mom (SAHM)?

In the 1950s, many American women stayed at home, took care of their kids and ran the household. The black-and-white image of an American housewife in an apron is a classic reflection of the cultural expectation.

Despite the feminist movement in the 1970s, the government did not implement policies to make it easy for women to work after having children. The *New York Times* published a hypothesis that the reason America's birth rate reached a historic low in 2017 is because the country fundamentally does not support working mothers.[35]

Additionally, public school education does not start until kindergarten. If both parents want to work, they have to send their children to private daycare facilities or hire a nanny for the first five years. The cost of childcare in the first five years is *not* trivial. According to *New America*, a think tank in Washington, D.C., the average cost of daycare in the US— $9,589 per year—edges out the average cost of in-state college tuition at $9,410.[36] In Silicon Valley, day care expenses could be as much as $24,000 per child per year. The cost of childcare for two or more kids could easily be more than the after-tax income of one parent.

With all these variables, it is not surprising that American women have to consider the option of being a stay-at-home mom versus returning to work.

Is it worth it to stay at home? As a former investment banker, I evaluate options through the lens of a financial model. It allows me to quantify the variables and compare the options in a highly rational manner. In this case, career net present value (career NPV) is a highly effective tool.

What Is a Career NPV?

You are probably familiar with the concept of the time value of money. A dollar today is worth more than a dollar tomorrow because of the uses to which it can be put in the intervening time (interest, investment in resources, etc). But how do you compare the investments you have to make in your children and your career today with the value of the cash flow you will receive from your career in the future?

In finance, NPV is a common methodology to evaluate present value of future cash flows at the required rate of return compared to your current investments. Career NPV is the present value of your cash flows from your career discounted at the rate of inflation compared to your childcare expenses.

Career NPV helps you to compare the outcomes from the various scenarios you are considering for your family and career. By looking at the income you will make from your career over the course of your lifetime and translating them to today's value, you will know which option is the most suitable for you. This gives you a long-term view of your life and your career.

How Do You Apply Career NPV?

The easiest way to calculate your career NPV is to enter the childcare costs and your income from your career year by year and use the *npv* function in an Excel spreadsheet. (See Exhibit 1.)

I will illustrate this by comparing two scenarios for a woman named Lucile.

Lucile was twenty-seven years old when she became pregnant with her first son. She delivered her baby boy at twenty-eight and thought about forgoing her data analyst job that pays $60,000 a year. Instead, she would take care of her son at home for the first four years, and her family would not have to pay the expenses for private childcare. Day care expenses are assumed to start at $35,000 and decrease as he gets older.

Daycare is generally more expensive in the first year than in later years. This is because daycare centers' primary costs are pegged to the child to teacher ratio. In California, daycare centers are required to keep a 4:1 child to staff ratio until children reach eighteen months. That ratio increases to 6:1 when children are between eighteen months to three years old.[37] That means that for the cost of one teacher, a center can generate income from six children instead of four if the children are older.

If she were to stay home, she would return when her son turned five and went to public kindergarten. For our purposes, year zero is the year that Lucile was pregnant at work, year one marks the first year of her son, and so on. We looked at her NPV until year ten.

In scenario one, Lucile stayed at home, so her childcare expenses were zero in year one. In the year before the birth, she would earn $60,000 for working while pregnant, but receive no income for the next four years as she devoted all her time to her son. In year five, her son would go to kindergarten and Lucile would find a job that pays $60,000, the same amount she was making before she had her child. We assumed a $10,000 salary increase every four years, and 25 percent to taxes every year. If we discount her future cash flows at the rate of inflation, her career NPV over the first ten years of her child's life would be $272,420 (See Exhibit 1).

In scenario two, Lucile decided to put her son in Little Flowers Daycare and pay $35,000 in the first year, $33,000 in the second, $31,000 in the third and $30,000 in the fourth year. Lucile would go back to work at the same company after having her son and continues to build her experience and knowledge in data analysis. In year five, she was assumed to receive a promotion and receive a salary increase of $10,000 per year. While she would barely save money during the four years of putting her son through private childcare, her income potential would increase as she accumulated more experience. Her career NPV over the first ten years of her child's life would be $370,094.

Exhibit 1. Comparison of Lucile's Career NPV: Stay at Home vs. Career Mom with One Child

Lucile's Age	27	28	29	30	31	32	33	34	35	36	37
1st Child's Age	Year 0	Year 1	Year 2	Year 3	Year 4	Year 5	Year 6	Year 7	Year 8	Year 9	Year 10
Scenario 1. Stay at Home											
Childcare Expenses	-	-	-	-	-	-	-	-	-	-	-
Income from Career	$60,000	-	-	-	-	$60,000	$60,000	$60,000	$60,000	$60,000	$60,000
Taxes	($15,000)	-	-	-	-	($15,000)	($15,000)	($15,000)	($15,000)	($15,000)	($15,000)
Cash Flow	$45,000	-	-	-	-	$45,000	$45,000	$45,000	$45,000	$45,000	$45,000
Discount Rate (=Rate of Inflation)	2.0%										
Scenario 1. NPV	**$272,420**										
Scenario 2. Career Mom with One Child											
Childcare Expenses	-	($35,000)	($33,000)	($31,000)	($30,000)	-	-	-	-	-	-
Income from Career	$60,000	$60,000	$60,000	$60,000	$60,000	$70,000	$70,000	$70,000	$70,000	$80,000	$80,000
Taxes	($15,000)	($15,000)	($15,000)	($15,000)	($15,000)	($17,500)	($17,500)	($17,500)	($17,500)	($20,000)	($20,000)
Cash Flow	$45,000	$10,000	$12,000	$14,000	$15,000	$52,500	$52,500	$52,500	$52,500	$60,000	$60,000
Discount Rate (=Rate of Inflation)	2.0%										
Scenario 2. NPV	**$370,094**										
Difference between Scenario 1 vs 2	**$97,674**										

Note: To download the NPV tool in excel, please go to www.expectingatwork.com.

By continuing to pursue her career, Lucile would increase her career value by $97,674 more than if she stayed at home. In the early years of her son's life, she wouldn't have much savings as the US does not have government-sponsored childcare programs until kindergarten. However, she would make a higher income in year five, given the experience from those first four years and the fact that her promotions were assumed to begin in year two instead of year nine.

Rather than simply looking at the short-term cost-benefit, Lucile decided to take a long-term view on her career and chose to not let motherhood take precedent over her career.

Stress Test Your Assumptions

Right off the bat, you are probably asking about the unknowns. What if this happens or that happens. The great thing about the career NPV calculation is that you can tweak the key assumptions based on your personal situation. You can run sensitivity analysis to test out more scenarios after you have done your initial calculation. The more you run, the better the data to use in your decision making.

There are a few assumptions that should definitely be stress tested.

Career Break Penalty: Women often experience difficulties in returning to work after career breaks. In a study published by the Center for Talent Innovation in 2010, researchers found that "nearly nine of out 10 SAHMs wanted to resume their careers. While 73% succeeded in returning to their careers, only 40% found full-time, mainstream work."[38] Even if women can find a full-time position, they may not be able to find a job with comparable pay compared to before they left their careers.

According to PricewaterhouseCoopers, three in five professional women returning to work are likely to move into lower-paid roles, experiencing an immediate earnings reduction of up to a third.[39] In the case of Lucile, if she were to stay at home, it would be much harder to get a similar job with the same pay. If she were to take a haircut of 33 percent on her salary, the gap between scenario one and two would widen to $173,094, earning more from scenario two this time.

Career Trajectory Stalls: Technological advancement is happening faster than ever. One's skillset can become outdated if they do not keep up with the changes. In Lucille's case, a lot of software tools have been developed to make the job of a data analyst much more efficient, so an analyst can free up time to do more advanced work. If Lucille were to take four years off, her excel skillset would not be sufficient to perform the same job. It would require training to get to the same level as someone who never took a break.

Career Break Lengthens with Number of Children: If a woman decides to stay at home, the more children she has, the longer her career break will likely become. The implications for salary difference between a mom who continues to advance in her career and a stay-at-home mom who returns to work are even more pronounced. On the surface, it may appear that you are saving twice as much in childcare costs when in fact the money lost from your career is even greater in the later years.

Depending on the field you are in, the difference in your Career NPV can be substantial. That means you might want to consider digging into some savings in the short term to reap the long-term benefits. Catherine, an assistant professor at a public research institution and a mother of two toddlers, shared that academia could be really hard to go back into if she took a break. She was determined to continue working and said, "Even if we go into debt now, it will get better so long as we ride it out. Within the next five to ten years, we can make the money back."

The bottom line is most women who stay at home to care for their children lose more money in the long run than they would have had to pay in childcare in the short term.

Working Mothers Are Great Role Models for Our Children

Contrary to the conventional wisdom that working mothers are bad for children, researchers at Columbia University found that "the overall effect of first-year maternal employment on child development is neutral." The study followed 1,364 children from birth through first grade. Children of working mothers behaved no differently on cognitive tests than the ones of stay-at-home mothers if their working mothers improved their family's financial situation and managed to seek high quality childcare. Working mothers who continue to remain sensitive to their children's needs also have a significantly positive impact on their children's development.[40]

Moreover, children, especially daughters, can benefit from having working mothers. Kathleen L. McGinn, the Cahners-Rabb Professor at HBS, analyzed survey responses from over 31,000 men and women from twenty-four developed nations and concluded that women raised by working mothers were more likely to have jobs, more likely to hold managerial responsibilities and more likely to earn a higher income than women of stay-at-home mothers.[41] Men raised by working mothers are more likely to contribute to household chores, which would support their spouses to work.

I had a firsthand experience from having a working mother myself. I was the product of a dual-income family: my dad worked for a large state-owned enterprise in China while my mom was a factory worker. Mao had just implemented the one-child policy, so my parents showered me with all their love.

In the first year after my birth, my mom took one year of maternity leave, after which she returned to work. Every morning my father rode his bike with me in the front and sent his precious only daughter to a state-sponsored daycare center. Few people in China had cars back then and bikes were the main means of transportation. That breeze of cold air on those crispy winter mornings feels so fresh and familiar to me, even to this day.

It was never a question that my mom would continue to work. After the Chinese Revolution and the establishment of the People's Republic of China in 1949, Mao proclaimed that "women hold up half the sky" to prove that women can be a tremendous resource outside the home. In 1982, Chinese women accounted for 49 percent of the total population and 43 percent of the entire workforce. [42] Women had one year of maternity leave with seventy-two days fully paid.

My mom told me, "Everyone went back to work after maternity leave, so people did not think about not going back." Since 1980, China's gross domestic product (GDP) grew from $220 billion to $11.8 trillion in 2016, and women were a significant contribution to this growth. [43]

When I was eleven years old, my mother and her colleagues decided to set up their own yarn manufacturing business and raised capital from family and friends. They found a factory location in Jingshan District, a suburban area forty-six miles from downtown Shanghai. They chose this location to keep the rent low, but the trade-off was that everyone had to live and work there during the week.

During those first three years of her start-up, my mom had to take a two-and-a-half hour bus ride on Sunday evening to go to the factory and came home on Friday evenings. During the week, my father took on all the childcare responsibilities in order to support my mom's entrepreneurial endeavor. While my mother was away, I helped my father cook, from scrambling eggs to mixing batter to making beef noodle soups. My cooking skills dramatically improved as I observed my father and practiced myself under his supervision.

If it had not been those years of training, I would not have had the skills and confidence to leave Shanghai to attend Dartmouth College in the US by myself. From there, I completed a trimester studying Spanish art and literature in Barcelona, international economics in Oxford and financial markets in Milan, which ultimately led me to my first job out of college in investment banking at Morgan Stanley in London, England.

My mother's hardworking character and her perseverance in her entrepreneurial pursuit made her a great role model for me.

In hindsight, I am so grateful to her for making the sacrifices she made in order to build a business that allowed her to support my college education financially. I also have an incredible respect for my father who supported her along the way to make it work.

You, too, will inevitably experience those tough moments where you wish you could be with your children. Even though you may not see the positive impact on your children right away, it will manifest itself in the long run.

What the Numbers Do Not Tell You

Of course, there are always stories not being told by the numbers.

1. *Career as an Important Piece of Our Identity:* For many of us, continuing to work has more than just a financial appeal. Having a career is a piece of our identity that we worked hard to create. After we obtain our degrees, we spend two-thirds of our waking hours putting our education to use, developing our professional network and making contributions toward something greater than ourselves.

2. *Continued Self-Development Opportunity:* Having a career is a way to continue to develop ourselves and to develop our teams for those moms in managerial positions. Emi Yoshikawa had her daughter, Evie, in late 2016. While she was on maternity leave, she found a unique opportunity at a blockchain start-up leading their partnership efforts with Asian financial institutions. A Japanese native, Emi had spent her career in financial services in both the US and Asia with an MBA from Harvard. She was the perfect fit for her company.

She would have to travel a lot between San Francisco and Asia and spend time away from her daughter. After consulting with her family and friends, she made a difficult decision to take on the role when her daughter was three months old.

"I could not be happier with this decision," she said. "Working after having children is a big commitment, and I derive so much satisfaction for taking the leap of faith." After she settled into her role, she took her daughter to Asia from time to time so that her parents could take care of her in Japan, which was a great bonding experience for both her parents and her daughter.

3. *Financial Freedom:* Making our own income also provides a great deal of financial freedom. Even if there are some short-term savings for trading your job for caring for you children, you would give up your own income and possibly miss out on contributions to a 401-K during those years.

   Michelle Bailey, Group Vice President and General Manager for IDC, points out, "being a mother doesn't mean you shouldn't be focused on making money." She explains that you can find support in different areas, including your partner, your parents, friends, HR and even your neighbors, if you want to it badly enough.

4. *Risk Management:* No one can predict the future, but our own financial stability affords us freedom and opportunities. During the 2008 financial crisis, Susan's husband lost his high-paying job at a hedge fund. Because they lost their sole source of income, they had to downsize their home and their children had to switch schools due to the move. Having dual-income could have alleviated some mortgage stress after an unexpected loss of income.

5. *Independence:* Employment can also mean independence and stability. If a woman who has chosen to stay at

home with her children ends up getting a divorce, it can become incredibly difficult both emotionally and financially for her to stand on her own feet.

6. *Division of Household Responsibilities:* Last but not least, having your own income gives you more power in negotiating household duties at home. All too often I have seen women share their frustrations with their spouses for not doing enough, as they are considered the full-time housekeeper plus nanny plus home chef.

In the Netflix original comedy, *Hard Knock Wife,* comedian Ali Wong does not hold back on the "relentless" realities of motherhood. "You get no 401-K, no coworkers—you're just in solitary confinement all day long with this human Tamagotchi that doesn't have a reset button, so the stakes are extremely high!"

Despite all the benefits of being a working mother, women often encounter "maternal wall bias" in the office. This stems from the deeply rooted culture that women should take care of kids at home. According to Pew, some 40 percent of Americans believe it is bad for our society if women work. [44] If they attempt to do both, they are trading off kids with competence and commitment. In a study on 716 women who had left the tech industry, more than 25 percent attributed it to the unsupportive culture. [45]

Coupled with the working culture is the inflexible work arrangements. The results-based work model supporting flexible work arrangements described by Sheryl Sandberg in *Lean In* is still not common in most businesses. This becomes challenging to work around especially when unforeseen circumstances with your child rise.

Finally, though, a mother's strong desire to care for her child full-time can definitely outweigh any financial superiority. Jane candidly shared that she had planned on working after having her second child. After finding out that her second child had developmental challenges, she decided to take a career break in order to take her son to the doctor for ongoing treatment every week. The health of her child was a real challenge and required her time and commitment. She is happy about the decision and wouldn't change it.

The decision to stay at home versus continuing to work is a difficult and personal one. While you do want to consider your NPV, the numbers don't tell the entire picture. Despite the financial benefits, there are other reasons to consider staying at home. Ultimately, every family is different so you choose what you think is best for your family and for yourself. The most important thing is to consider all aspects of both sides and weigh them accordingly.

◊◊◊

Career NPV can serve as a tool for you to measure the long-term financial impact. To fully capture the value of your career requires you to persevere and work smart to develop a plan.

Remember those early years are hard, no matter which path you choose, but once you make the decision, feel good about it and make it work.

In the next section, you will learn about the challenges of a working mother, a set of strategies to overcome them and the mind shift required to execute those strategies.

Hey, it's Vivienne here and I'm the author of the book.

I hope you're enjoying it so far, finding it both relatable and practical. **I have a favor to ask you. Would you consider giving it a rating on Amazon, please?** My goal is for this book to be considered a must-read for new working moms, and one way to help establish the book's status is a boat-load of Amazon love that speaks to why it's valued.

Many thanks in advance,

My goal is for this

Photo: My daughters, Genevieve and Josephine, and me.

Section III.

Mindful Return

Chapter 8.

A Structured Approach to Your New Work Life

W hen you return to work, you will be establishing a new routine. Between ramping up at work, frequent pumping, sleep training and managing childcare for your new baby, it is not unusual to feel overwhelmed.

The constant struggle to maintain a family and a job makes us question our ability to do both well. In the *New York Times*, columnist Lisa Belkin coined the term "Opt-Out Revolution" to describe high achieving women who had achieved their career success and left their fields after becoming mothers. She attributed this trend partially to women feeling that they could not dedicate themselves fully to their job or their family.[46]

From my interviews with career moms, I have found a common pattern: these women all take a structured approach to defining their own success at work and at home. Rather than measuring themselves against others, they set up specific goals tailored to their own family and professional lives. By establishing their own success parameters regularly, they feel a great level of satisfaction when they achieve them.

Kelli Moles, associate partner at McKinsey and a mother of three, decided to "do McKinsey on her own terms" rather than opting out. Upon returning to work after her second child, she realized that she could not do everything she used to do at work, such as staying past eight in the evening every day. So she decided to develop a set of goals and aimed to achieve them every week. For example, she does bedtime with her children four times a week, which frees her up to attend one client dinner on the day that she misses bedtime. She made compromises and set clear boundaries between home and work, which she communicated and stood by.

With this approach, she feels confident in her new life and can easily make trade-off decisions on her own terms. Her firm decided to put her up for partner while she was on maternity leave with her third son.

Define Your Structure

As you prepare to return to work, you should try to structure your own approach to your new work and family life. Here is a set of advice from the career moms I interviewed.

1. *Find a Good Caregiver or Daycare:* A good caregiver or daycare will spare you a lot of worries. References from your local mothers' clubs and your mommy tribe at work can be an excellent way to source your caregiver. Several online services, such as Care.com, also provide a network of care providers for you to connect with. From interviewing to background checks, it could take several weeks or months to find someone you trust. Start this process early because good care can be hard to find.

2. *Put Your Baby on a Schedule:* Prior to returning to work, you might want to put your baby on a schedule. Babies love routines and tend to develop a better sleeping pattern with them. We closely followed the guidelines from Lucie's List (www.*lucieslist.com*) one month prior

to my return to work. It took two weeks for Genevieve to sleep through the night, allowing me to rest well during the work week.

3. *Discuss Your Re-Entry with Your Manager*: Discuss your responsibilities approximately two weeks prior to your return. Your business and team may have evolved during your leave. Through discussions, you can review and modify the re-entry plan based on your own and your business needs. A two-week window gives you time to iterate the plan a few times to a satisfying state, but doesn't force re-entry prematurely.

4. *Set Specific Weekly Goals as a Good Mom and Employee*: Think about what goals will make you feel good as a new mom and employee, respectively. Setting specific goals can help erase the feeling of guilt from having to miss a client dinner for story time with your child, because you choose to stick to your own goals. Clients and story time are not in competition if you've identified your goals ahead of time.

5. *Set Your Own Boundaries*: It is helpful to set your own boundaries and make them known to others at work. Nicole, a marketing director at a bank, has to leave work at 4:30 p.m. to pick up her child from day care and then makes herself available over email after 8:30 p.m. when her child goes to bed. She shares that constraint with her team so her team does not schedule calls past 4:30 p.m. Being upfront allows you and others around to plan work effectively.

6. *Schedule Your Own Pumping Breaks*: Meetings will get scheduled if your calendar is free. Blocking off the times in your calendar is an effective way to free yourself up for pumping.

Returning to work from maternity leave is one of the most important transitions in your career. At times, you will feel overwhelmed and completely exhausted. There are going to be days when your nanny is sick and you have to find a back-up on short notice, or when your husband is out of town, leaving you to handle your child's sleep regression alone.

I have experienced this firsthand and so have many other career moms. Do not be afraid to reach out for help and advice to your work tribe, your local mothers' club and the *Expecting at Work* Facebook group. You can benefit from our collective knowledge and you *will* get through it.

My Job Changed And So Did I

After I had my first daughter, I went back to work after ten weeks. My mom stayed with us for five months to help look after Genevieve, so I felt at ease when it came to childcare.

I had a manager who was relatively new to the business, so he was still getting accustomed to our business cadence when I returned. In the first week, I jumped straight into the fire by leading a quarterly ops review with our VP in Europe. Typically, I would spend three weeks working on it with the general managers of different business units, but we only had one week to work on it as our VP moved up his travel schedule. Of course, I ended up working all weekend and bringing my manager up to speed the first week after I returned.

Within the first two months of my return, I led the annual long-range planning process for six business units across sales, marketing, technology and operations. I also traveled to Amsterdam to attend a conference and delivered a presentation to 250 people, where I had to frantically run back to my hotel room from the conference center to pump because there was no mothers' room.

On an eleven-hour flight back to San Francisco from Amsterdam, I needed to pump mid-flight and a very nice Dutch flight attendant allowed me to use the nook designated as their rest area. I closed the curtain, put together the pumping gears and started the machine.

As the sound of the breast pump faded into the background, I stared at the blank wall and tears fell down my cheeks.

For the first time, I had been away from my four-month-old daughter for five days straight. I missed her. I was sad I wasn't there to watch her sit up for the first time. I wanted to be there to read to her in Chinese and play peek-a-boo with her.

But deep down I knew that wasn't the real reason I cried.

Something had changed. I had been excited for this trip. I'd always enjoyed traveling for work. It was actually one of the reasons I was drawn to the job in the first place. Having worked and lived on three continents, I loved working with a diverse group of people and learning from each other. After this trip, I realized I no longer derived satisfaction from that aspect of my job.

I was terrified.

I had changed. What used to be a perk at my job became a burden. I would rather spend my time creating direct value for the business than traveling eleven hours. Time had become such a precious gift that I wanted to make every minute count.

Because I chose to spend a big chunk of my time away from my daughter, I wanted to maximize the value I created for the business, for my family and for myself. It was important for me to "get on a rocket ship"[47] where companies are growing quickly and making a lot of impact. I wanted to work for a business that cared about giving back to the community.

Learning to prioritize my own needs with those of my company allowed me to become fearless in the pursuit of a satisfying career.

I'm not the only one who has faced shifting priorities. It is common for mothers to re-evaluate their jobs and prospects. It's important to vocalize those needs to make it work.

Pam worked in mergers and acquisitions (M&A) for ten years before she had her child. Upon her return from maternity leave, she spent a lot of time actively prospecting M&A deals in a new field. She was less concerned about the childcare expenses than the value she could be creating from those hours. While she was excited about leading new projects, these new projects did not fit with the direction of her company.

Pam wanted to make every minute count. "Every single minute I spend at work is a minute I could have spent with my daughter," she said. Encouraged by her manager, she went on to start her own smart energy business. She aimed to solve a problem she had seen from her previous work experience and to create a meaningful impact in her industry.

Of course, a shift in priorities does not necessarily mean changing jobs or changing companies. Rather, it is a change in attitude toward our work—our fearless pursuit of a job that will satisfy us.

What Doesn't Change

Contrary to the traditional beliefs, motherhood does not temper a woman's ambition. In a 2017 study by Accenture, researchers found that women with children are as likely as women without children to aspire to senior leadership roles. Mothers are more likely to change jobs for a promotion or higher pay.

We have seen an increasing number of self-made, new moms making it into the headlines. In 2018, Katrina Lake, CEO of Stitch Fix, took the company public on NASDAQ Stock Market fourteen months after her son was born. She made it a point to hold her son at the podium of the exchange because she felt people needed to see mothers could excel at work. Michelle Zatlyn, COO of Cloudflare, grew the company to over one billion dollar valuation within three years of becoming a mother of two. Jennifer Hyman, CEO of Rent the Runway, continued to grow the fashion rental business and create shareholder value after having her daughter. *Working Mother* magazine even put together a list of the 50 Most Powerful Moms last year, to celebrate and inspire all of us.[48]

Not only do our ambitions not change but our skills don't go away. In fact, we become more skillful at our jobs and at our homes, making us better leaders in businesses. Here are the four key skills that many experienced moms have mastered to make everything work. When you're thinking about the benefits of motherhood, don't forget these.

1. *Ruthless Prioritization.* With one more person to take care of, the amount of work at home piles up very quickly; thus, it is no longer possible to do everything to perfection while staying sane. Instead, you have to pick and choose what is the most important to be at 100 percent and leave the rest at 70 percent or less. And it is a constant prioritization and re-prioritization.

   Christa, CEO of OpenTable, had two kids while working as a top-performing Wall Street analyst. She shared that her best stock picks were after she became a mother. She had the laser focus to filter out the noise and focus on what matters most.

2. *Efficiency and Productivity.* In a 2014 study conducted by the Federal Reserve Bank of St. Louis, researchers found a positive correlation between motherhood and productivity.[49] Notably, working mothers with two or more children are more productive than mothers of one child. Working mothers in general are more productive than women without children. The constant juggling and multitasking skills at home are transferable to work and make us more efficient, productive workers.

3. *Empathetic Leadership.* During my interviews with experienced mothers, almost all agreed that becoming a mother developed their ever-growing appreciation for other working parents. This increased empathy allowed us to ask questions that we might have not thought about previously, reducing our blind spots.

Sheryl Sandberg shared the story of her request to put in parking spots dedicated to pregnant mothers closer to the Google campus when she became pregnant herself. Her awareness of others' needs increased because of her own motherhood experience, making her a better leader. Expert in inspirational leadership Simon Sinek explains, "Empathy—the ability to recognize and share other people's feelings—is the most important instrument in a leader's toolbox."

4. *Courage and Assertiveness.* Oxytocin is one of the key hormones in bonding a mother and a child. Neurologists found an increase in oxytocin in birthing mothers during pregnancy and postpartum. In 2014, researchers at the University of Bonn Hospital show that this bonding hormone inhibits the fear center in the brain and allows fear stimuli to subside more easily.[50] Our protective instincts are less susceptible to fear and we become more courageous.

Amy Henderson, Co-Founder of Tend Lab which was designed to unlock the power of parenthood at work, shared a story of a senior programmer becoming more assertive with her direct reports on the quality of their work after she became a mother. Her newly developed courage allowed her to be much more effective at work.

Motherhood is an amazing training ground for leadership development. Our ability to collaborate well with others in a focused and productive manner makes us an invaluable asset in the workplace.

Make Your Job Work for You

With all the changes in you and the workplace, what does that leave for you?

In a recent survey, I reached out to US-based working mothers on Facebook and asked what they think companies could do to help retain new moms. Out of the 216 responses, 92.1 percent of women selected "flexible work arrangements," followed by "gradual return to work program" by 78.6 percent of women.

Some companies actually have the "gradual return to work" as a benefit for new moms. At Salesforce, not only do we get twenty-six weeks of paid parental leave but we have a gradual return-to-work program where returning mothers work four days a week in the first month to help ease the transition.

A colleague of mine, Molly Branch, came back from her maternity leave and shared how much she appreciated this program. "It has helped me integrate rather than jumping back in cold turkey, and I appreciate that it's a company policy, so I didn't have to fight for it."

It is in companies' benefit to take a long-term view and implement policies that make it easy for mothers to continue working. In the "CS Gender 3000: Progress in the Boardroom," researchers found that "investors focusing on those companies where gender diversity is an important factor in their strategy continue to be rewarded with excess returns running at a CAGR of 3.5 percent."

Sampada Telang, a long-term Googler who specializes in Partnerships, joined the company when she was four months pregnant. She had been working at an advertising start-up for a couple of years, but was offered a role at Google that was a perfect fit for her skills. Despite being new at Google, when Sampada disclosed her pregnancy to her manager, he was fully supportive. He encouraged her to take advantage of Google's generous maternity benefits and take the time off to bond with the newborn, even though it meant he would lose 50% of his team for five months. She took the full leave and returned to work energized to pick up where she left off.

A great company will not turn you away because of your gender, race and ethnicity.

If you are at a company without these stated benefits, you can still make it work. It will require more time and energy, but you only have more to lose for not ever trying.

Consider taking the following approaches:

1. *Work with Your Manager:* Your manager can be your closest ally and strongest advocate. You have earned your equity and built trust by doing great work in the past. It is mutually beneficial for you two to come up with an arrangement that works for both. Recall that it costs 20 percent of a person's annual salary to replace a worker. Hiring takes a great deal of effort and it takes even more time to train someone new.

   As in any negotiation, you will want to research what has been done in the past, decide what is the most important for you and prioritize, so you can have a meaningful discussion.

2. *Liaise with Your Expecting at Work Tribe:* Hopefully by now you have built rapport with a group of expecting moms

at work. This is when your tribe can come together and help one another. You can also learn tips on how to simplify and automate tasks to work more efficiently.

More importantly, you have the power of the group. Share with each other what you and your managers have worked out, so you have real examples and data points to strengthen your points of view.

3. *Consult with HR*: Some companies do not have certain policies simply because management is unaware of the needs. By researching and collecting examples of policies that work, you could propose new policy changes. Some women do not feel comfortable doing this on their own, but you can join forces with your tribe and ask for changes collectively.

I have seen women working in law, accounting, consulting, government work and other fields manage to work out various arrangements. Valerie, a product manager and new mother, worked with her manager to agree on an arrangement for redistributing the one month maternity leave to a four-day per work week for the first six months.

Furthermore, we have entered into a new era of work with the widespread adoption of network technology. In a networked and interconnected world, we can connect to our work more conveniently than ever before.

Jane Greenthal, a senior design strategist at Gensler and a mother of three, took a career break to stay at home with her children after having her second child in the late 1990s. At the time, it was not possible to work virtually, which would have helped alleviate some logistical burdens of having multiple young children. She pointed out the internet has transformed the way we work in the last decade, making it possible to work remotely with some flexibility.

The digital age enables a new way of working. Employers may not have changed their policies to adapt to the changing work environment, but it is definitely worth some negotiation to make it work.

If you have tried to make it work at your company in vain, it is worthwhile to know the key players with a more supportive culture in your industry. The website Fairygodboss can help you get the inside scoop on pay, corporate culture, benefits and work flexibility, so you can find a great company to work for. Networking with other mothers in a similar industry or function could also help you identify those players.

The best companies come up with policies to attract the best talent. It is on you to find who they are and go after them.

Your career is a long-term investment and takes a lot of effort. Those early years of motherhood will be challenging to manage from a financial, time and resources perspective. But by making it work, you will reap the benefits in the long run.

◊◊◊

As a mother of two daughters, I want to help shape corporate America so my daughters do not have to ask for policies that should exist in the first place. If every single one of us is vocal about our needs, collectively we can and will move it forward. We do this not only for ourselves but for our fellow moms and for our future generations.

In the next chapter, I will share with you one of the major challenges that many women face when they return to work.

You might be inclined to believe that special arrangements at work aren't necessary, or that you want to "blend in" as quickly as you can, but you will very likely need an optimal setup after you return from maternity leave. Not only is it helpful for you to be aware of this now but you will want to form allies to make it easier to overcome this challenge.

Chapter 9.

The Every-Three-Hour Routine

E arly one January morning in 1999, Cathy was leafing through an investor presentation while pumping breast milk in her office. She was about to begin a year-end conference call with investors to review her company's performance over the past year.

Suddenly, a window cleaner descended and began wiping her window outside the forty-floor high rise.

"Oh my God!" Caught by surprise, she immediately grabbed the newspaper by her desk to cover herself up from a man coming out of nowhere.

Like Cathy, many new mothers choose to continue pumping breast milk after they return to work. It is not uncommon to hear about those "surprise visits" from mothers in the workplace.

Thanks to the Affordable Care Act in 2010, employers are now required to provide working mothers with lactation rooms for pumping. According to the law, this must be "a place, other than a bathroom, that is shielded from view and free from intrusion from coworkers and the public."[51]

Lactation rooms vary greatly in terms of quality and care. Some companies have the bare minimum: a lockable room, a chair, a fridge for milk storage and some cubbies for storing supplies. Others really up the ante to make women feel welcome, hence easing the letdown by adding a mirror, a stocked magazine rack, a sink and Kleenex boxes. Almost all have whiteboards so that mothers can leave notes for each other and pin up baby photos if they'd like.

At Salesforce, we can book the lactation rooms online in advance. There is even a hospital-grade Medela pump in every room, eliminating the need for mothers to bring their own pumps. With my first daughter, I remember getting so tired of having to lug my breast pump back and forth from home to my previous employer every day that I ended up buying an additional pump solely for work.

Providing a hospital-grade pump shows how thoughtful and forward-thinking leaders are at a company. "It's not just the right thing to do, it's the smart thing to do," Stitch Fix CEO Katrina Lake said.

By easing women's return to work, it generates much more productivity and loyalty.

Make Your Manager a Great Manager

Breastfeeding becomes more difficult after you return to work because scheduling is a challenge. Depending on when you return to work, you may have to pump for fifteen to twenty minutes every three hours to maintain milk production. From setting up to pumping, storing milk in bags to cleaning up, it could take up to thirty minutes each time.

With my first daughter, I returned to work after ten weeks. At the time, my supply had just been established and I had to pump at least every three hours in order to keep up the flow.

One day, I was in a five-hour planning meeting with a room full of men. I distinctly remember the pain of being engorged with no relief. But the last thing I wanted to do was to call a break. I didn't want to be seen as a new mom – not committed to work.

Eventually, our COO, Ron Jaiven, a father of two with a working wife, stood up and asked that we take a break. I was desperate for a chance to run to the lactation room. Knowing that I had a short window, I immediately rushed to the fourth floor from the tenth floor with my bag of supplies. I was so relieved when I finally got the chance to pump.

Later, I thanked Ron for calling a break. He told me in private that because his wife had gone through something similar, he figured I could probably use a break to "take care of business."

I love telling people this story for three reasons.

1. By sharing yourself and bringing your full self to work, you can build allies at work who can help you. In my case, I had mentioned to Ron previously that my baby was still on breast milk when I first returned to work. He took note of this information and made my return-to-work experience much easier.

2. Great managers are the ones who take it to the next level by asking questions and showing a great level of empathy by acting on those new insights. Ron was aware of my unspoken needs and took action to help me. The fact that his wife was a working wife helped increase his awareness.

3. Your decision to work not only impacts you, but the people around you. It makes a difference to other women in the workplace. Your colleagues become more empathetic toward your fellow working mothers who

are trying to not let motherhood derail their careers. By sharing your challenges with your spouse, you also help him become more aware of a new working mother's needs, enabling him to provide support to his female direct reports when they return from maternity leave.

Sally, a product strategy manager, returned to work after a four-month maternity leave. While she was on leave, a company reorganization happened. Luckily she was able to continue working for the same manager. Her manager assigned her to a brand-new product that the company was launching in a month, which she was very excited about.

On day one, she eagerly attended an initial meeting with her product counterparts. To her surprise, she was told that the project was already one month behind schedule. Her counterparts had raised this issue with the manager several times prior to her return, but he did not make any progress or staffing arrangements. He simply assumed that Sally was going to make up for the lost time right after maternity leave. He did not set Sally up for success.

During the month leading up to the product release, Sally worked non-stop and lived on four–five hours of sleep every night. Her milk supply plummeted like an inverse hockey stick, forcing her to stop breastfeeding immediately. Despite being a father of two, Sally's manager was completely unaware of the difficulties that women encounter after maternity leave because his wife stayed home and did not have the same challenges.

One does not have to have children and a working wife to be a great manager. However, as working mothers, we influence managers to go from good to great by standing up as examples and sharing our experiences.

Realize That Less is Better Than None

"Breast is best" shows up everywhere we go, from pregnancy check-ups to pediatrician's offices. Everyone knows the benefits of breast milk, commonly referred to as "liquid gold." Most mothers plan to breastfeed. However, external factors like having no maternity leave or an unwelcoming working environment make it challenging to follow the recommendations.

Stress is a main cause for decreased milk production. Between meetings, reports, analyses and emails, it can be disruptive to leave your work for thirty minutes. Deadlines or frequent fire drills can cause a high level of stress. Some women have to stop breastfeeding earlier than they plan because their work is too stressful and supply does not keep up.

Not all careers are conducive to a regular pumping schedule. A senior trader at a hedge fund returned to work after two weeks and had to put her son on formula immediately. Working in a male-dominant environment, she was the only female trader and mother on the trading floor. Leaving her desk to pump during market open meant possibly losing hundreds of thousands of dollars for the firm. Instead of completely giving up, she pumped in the evenings and on weekends.

"Less is better than none," she said to me. "And even if I have none, it is still not the end of the world."

According to Centers for Disease Control, 81 percent of mothers across America reported breastfeeding at some point, but it decreases to about 22 percent when looking at exclusive breastfeeding for six months, a recommendation by the American Academy of Pediatrics.[52] Despite the low rate of exclusive breastfeeding, we still have healthy kids on formula.

When I talked to my mom about stopping breastfeeding at six months, she let me in on a big secret. In the late 1970s and 1980s, China went through economic reform and opened its door to the rest of the world. During that time, Western formula was introduced and marketed as a rare, nutritious food for infants.

This was the beginning of one-child policy where parents were willing to invest big into that one child. People stormed into stores to buy that precious formula. You would often see a line out the door buying formula. Monique, who lives in the Netherlands, told me that even today Chinese people buy so much HiPP Dutch formula that the manufacturer cannot keep up. The Dutch government has to limit each visitor to two boxes of formula per visit to the store.

Not surprisingly, I was brought up on that formula along with many others. We are healthy and have done well for ourselves.

"The happiest new moms are the ones who do not breastfeed," my lactation consultant shared with me. There is a lot of truth to it. As mothers, we often put so much pressure on ourselves to follow breastfeeding recommendations that we make significant sacrifices to make it work.

A happy mom is just as important to a healthy child as our "liquid gold." Doing the best we can is great, but it cannot come at the cost of our own healthy, stable mental state. Our kids will grow up with or without breast milk.

◊◊◊

Even pumped breast milk, although it will nourish and fill up the baby, will not bond you and the baby the same way as if she takes breast milk directly. As new working mothers, this is just one of the many internal conflicts with which we struggle and is part of the "relentless prioritization" I mentioned in Chapter 8.

There will be many more such conflicts, but they are all part of becoming the best person you can be. In the following chapter, I will reveal the biggest conflict one may face regarding childcare. You will learn about the empirical studies regarding this conflict as well as the insights and secrets of experienced career moms.

Chapter 10.

My Daughter Prefers the Nanny

W hen my daughter was five months old, I had already been back to work for two-and-a-half months. Since my mom had to go back to China, due to the six-month limit on visitor visas in the US, we had to make childcare arrangements for my daughter, Genevieve.

As a native Chinese, I wanted my children to grow up speaking Mandarin and to learn the same Chinese songs and traditions that I had. Their ethnicity is an important part of their identity and I wanted them to understand it. Their educational influence is a high priority for me in addition to their safety and health. But we were living in a predominantly Caucasian neighborhood and there was no Mandarin bilingual daycare center.

Having a nanny would be more expensive, but we wanted Gen to have more one-on-one attention at such a young age. The higher expense would only be for a short time and we had mentally prepared ourselves for it.

After speaking to several new Chinese parents, we decided to hire a Chinese live-in nanny.

There are many benefits to having a live-in nanny. First, a live-in nanny is often older with more childcare experience and is fully dedicated to your child. Unlike an au pair, many of these nannies have had children themselves. Not only do they have firsthand childcare experience, but they have worked as childcare providers for other young families. When it comes to a young, fragile infant, experience matters.

Second, a nanny can help with basic chores like cooking and cleaning which are not directly childcare-related. The cost of a live-in is less than a regular nanny because free room and board is included in the employment agreement.

Finally, you don't have to worry about pickups and drop-offs, which are time consuming. From dressing her to feeding her and getting her in the car seat, it can take thirty minutes to one hour every morning. Not having to worry about picking her up by a certain time in the evening offers great flexibility for your career. Even though a live-in nanny can compromise your privacy, it may be worth the trade-off for great childcare and convenience.

For us, the additional benefit was that she would speak Mandarin to our daughter 24/7. Since Jacob does not speak any Mandarin, having someone who could converse in Mandarin with me would immerse Genevieve in a Mandarin-speaking environment.

Once we had made up our minds to have a live-in nanny, we embarked on a search for one. Having someone come and live with your family is not a trivial decision. I had prepared a long list of interview questions to gauge the person's experience and trustworthiness.

We posted an advertisement in the Bay Area Chinese newspaper. Over the course of several weeks, we interviewed over twenty-four candidates over the phone and had two in-person interviews. After seeing how Anna cared for our five-month-old Genevieve, we chose her.

Anna was a sixty-year-old Chinese woman whose daughter lives in Singapore. She moved to the Bay Area by herself and acquired her green card five years ago. She had worked for three families and cared for children ranging between six months and four years old. She spoke Mandarin to Genevieve, sang Chinese songs, and fed her delicious home-cooked meals.

Anna treated Gen like her own daughter and Genevieve grew increasingly attached to her. I never worried about leaving Genevieve to go to work. I could not have been happier with this arrangement until one day when I had returned from a business trip in Seattle. One-year-old Genevieve had had a breakdown because her cracker had broken into pieces as she was playing with it. Both Anna and I rushed over to her to make sure she was okay.

With two of us standing in front of her, she opened her arms to Anna instead of me! Anna comforted her immediately and burst into laughter pretty soon after that.

I could not fall asleep that night. "Why does Genevieve prefer Anna? Have I made a mistake by hiring her? What if Genevieve does not love me?"

"They Can Always Have More People to Love"

It is not uncommon to be concerned that someone else is taking care of your children or that you are not spending enough time with them. After all, as working mothers, we spend the majority of the day at work. Between the commute and work, we can spend up to ten hours away from our children during the week. That only leaves us with breakfast time in the morning, dinner time and bedtime in the evening, totaling no more than three hours a day, or four hours at best.

As our young babies spend the majority of their waking hours with their caregivers, it is only normal, in fact better, if they grow attached to the caregivers. Trust builds over time. The more time a baby spends with someone, the more likely that the baby considers that person the most trusted person. On the flip side, if the baby is not well cared for, they have the instincts to reject the person in order to protect themselves.

The fact that Genevieve was growing increasingly attached to her nanny was only a positive signal that Gen trusted and loved Anna.

Baily Kempner shared her story about her return to work after three months. She had hired her nanny to take care of her first son Tom. She had always wanted to develop her career while building a family, but it was still challenging to leave her son with someone for an extended period of time.

She shared an insight from her mother that has stuck with me. "They can always have more people to love." Her point was that starting at a young age, the kids are surrounded by parents, grandparents, extended families and others. The more kids give their love, the more they receive love.

According to the Children and Young People's Mental Health Coalition, babies use their relationships with others to set up an expectation about themselves.[53] Having loving relationships with more than one person helps children develop the social skills to form bonds with others early on. Moreover, children who are securely attached are better able to manage their own feelings and behaviors and better able to relate to others.

Having a great nanny that your child loves also makes it easier for us to return to work. Rather than spending our energy worrying for our children, we can focus on making the most of our working hours.

Lisa Edwards of Salesforce shared that she had her son through IVF without a spouse. With no close families around, she hired a manny to take care of her son after she went back to work. Because she was a single mother, her manny was able to take care of some heavy lifting duties in addition to the regular childcare. The amount of support she was able to get from him allowed her to dive straight back into work.

Within six months of her return, Lisa was asked to build out a business development team at Visa. Having commitment and talent is one thing. Having trusted support at home enables one to unleash all the potential at work.

You are still their mother and have a place in their life even with a nanny. With limited time after work, I made sure to have alone time with Genevieve for thirty minutes in the evenings. I plan a special activity for us to do during that time. Sometimes we watch seagulls and stroll by the ocean. I have made my own puppet theater show for her. To her, mommy always provides fun and new activities and she looks forward to our time together. It was important for me to make those memorable experiences with her.

Stress Quality over Quantity

My favorite fitness trainer is the inventor of P90X, Tony Horton. I started doing P90X after I gave birth to Genevieve because of its in-home video feature. I chose this program because it is a system designed to strengthen one's overall fitness, like speed, strength, flexibility and muscle growth in ninety days.

One of the things Tony stresses is "quality over quantity" for strength training, meaning that your posture matters significantly to the effectiveness of the training.

The same philosophy applies to our children. Quality time spent with your children trumps quantity. Emily Chang, Bloomberg TV anchor and a mother of three, said, "When I'm home with my son, I make it count. When I'm at work, I make it count."[54]

Contrary to traditional belief, there is no positive correlation between time spent with children and their future success. According to a large-scale, longitudinal study of American families, time spent with parents between the ages of three and eleven had essentially nothing to do with how children turned out. Sociologist Melissa Milkie remarked, "I could literally show you 20 charts, and 19 of them would show no relationship between the amount of parents' time and children's outcomes. ... Nada. Zippo."[55]

Still, we like to beat ourselves up for not spending enough time with our children. The truth is that there is no magic formula for the amount of time spent with our children and their success. This "never enough" mentality causes more stress and guilt, which can have negative impacts on our children. According to Milkie's research, one key instance when parent time can be particularly harmful to children is when parents, mothers in particular, are stressed, sleep-deprived, guilty and anxious.

Amy, a marketing executive at a healthcare company, gave birth to twin boys and continued to work after giving birth. When they were five months old, she had to travel from the east coast to the west coast for a two-day healthcare conference. She had always considered herself a career woman but was surprised at "being overwhelmed with the feeling of guilt" throughout her trip.

That feeling distracted her from being 100 percent present at the conference. After she returned home, she found herself trying to do everything she could for the infants and watching over her nanny's shoulder as her nanny cared for the twins. She even had small arguments with the nanny in the twins' presence.

When she shared her story, she realized that she was bouncing back and forth between beating herself up at work and at home. Instead, she needed to make every minute count, and be 100 percent in the thing that she is doing, whether at home or at work.

Milkie's study further shows that "income and a mother's educational level are most strongly associated with a child's future success." By contributing to household income, working mothers can seek high quality childcare and relieve families of financial stress.

"You are always going to be the mother," Christa affirmed, as she shared her love for her kids' nanny. That will never change. Our sense of guilt only has a negative impact on our children, which is the opposite of what we want for them.

The next time those negative feelings occur, think about what you want for your child and remind yourself that guilt or insecurity does not help you get to your goal.

Working mothers are great role models for children. There will be times when our plans fall apart and our decision to work comes into question. We can practice and strengthen the muscles to have the confidence in our choice for ourselves, our children and our workplaces.

Chapter 11.

Final Reflections

On a Sunday evening, we had finally put both kids to bed after a full day of screaming and crying.

My parents had just left for Shanghai because my dad had to go back for major surgery. We were on our own with a two-and-a-half-year-old and a two-month-old with no help. Earlier in the morning, Genevieve had awakened with a rash all over her body and was scratching herself. Jacob had to rush her to urgent care. I stayed home with our two-month-old daughter, Josephine, so she wouldn't be exposed to germs in the hospital.

Just after they returned from the urgent care with the diagnosis of simple heat rash, I started to prepare lunch for all of us. As I was cutting some scallions, I noticed a giant lump forming around my wrist and it felt sore. In order to let Gen rest, I went to the emergency room by myself in fear of a fracture or something unknown. Jacob stayed home with both kids. He called it "one man down."

I feared going to the ER by myself. What if they discovered some incurable disease or had to do surgery? An X-ray and multiple check-ups later, the ER doctor diagnosed that I had developed a ganglion cyst, commonly found in women between ages twenty and forty with unknown reasons. I was relieved that it was not a fractured bone because I could hardly imagine being able to attend to both kids with one arm…

After speaking to Jacob on the phone, we decided to leave the cyst as was in hope of it subsiding on its own rather than having the doctor drain it. Having been at the ER for several hours, I was in a rush to go home and breastfeed Josie.

"What a day!" We finally had some quiet time to relax on the couch, completely exhausted. It had been one of those days that any parent would dread: health issues with one kid and one parent, screaming baby with no mother around and daddy being home alone with both kids.

"How are you doing?" I asked Jacob, concerned that both kids might have drained his patience.

Jacob turned to me and said, "You know, I had a decent day today. It was so tiring but our daughters melt my heart." He went on to describe how Genevieve carefully put the blanket onto her two-month-old sister singing "Twinkle Twinkle Little Star" as soon as she heard Josephine crying.

Because I was away, Jacob witnessed a maturing side to our older daughter.

While our day was filled with unexpected visits to the doctors, we managed to see the beautiful side of it.

We chose to have kids. Not just one, but two. Life became more complicated with all the logistics. Even going to the grocery store involves coordination with my partner and planning the best timing. Sometimes those days feel long, stressful and messy.

Vivian Greene says it best, *"Life isn't about waiting for the storm to pass . . . It's about learning to dance in the rain."*

Photo: Our first family outing when Josie was two-and-a-half months old.

◊◊◊

Saying that having a baby is no easy task is a vast understatement. At a first-time coffee chat with several new first-time moms, a mother of a ten-week-old remarked with a smile when asked how she was doing, "I only cried twice in the last week!" She said it in such a light tone that we all laughed with her. Deep inside, we all knew we would go through very similar experiences. Her candid comment bonded us instantaneously and we took turns sharing our breakdown moments.

To survive and thrive as working mothers, we need *real* friendships. They are not the ones you see on TV where the house is in perfect order, the mother has the perfect nails and the babies are always smiling like angels.

Real friendships are the ones where you risk yourself by sharing your struggles as you figure out this motherhood thing, and your friend nods and shares their struggles. It is like looking into a mirror. You decide to be *real* and the other person reciprocates. Only by being open and vulnerable can we have authentic conversations to support and motivate each other.

◇◇◇

Having children is one of the hardest things we do to our bodies.

When you care and love this new life so much, it is easy to forget about your own needs. You put a lot of pressure to raise your children well. That is all great, but the only sustainable way to do all these things well is to have self-care first.

Go ahead and schedule your monthly brunch with your girlfriends, your weekly workouts and even just fifteen minutes to decompress by yourself. Loving yourself is the foundation before you can love anyone else.

◇◇◇

Lastly, not all jobs are the same. You may have done the same job at the same company for a long time before you had your baby. Chances are that your criteria for a good job have changed after such a life-changing event. If your criteria are not met, you do not have to quit the job.

You can always ask for what you want and see if it works out. What is there to lose, really? I have seen numerous women work with their managers and HR to figure out a plan that works for all parties. Even if it does not work out, there are great companies with pioneering policies that support mothers with careers. If you love what you do, it is worthwhile to explore your options and make it work.

Being a trailblazer takes time and effort, but you will be paving a path forward for yourself and your children.

"It is not broken to be a software developer, a happy-go-lucky young woman, a mother of two kids and a c-suite executive all at once. *What is broken is that this is unusual at all,*" said Bridget Frey, CTO of Redfin and mom of two boys. "We have to make room for women to be all of these things at once without being crushed by that excruciating pressure to fit into a box that someone else made. We need to start first by making room in just one woman, inside ourselves."

Enjoy this beautiful and yet challenging ride! Keep looking for joy amidst all the chaos.

About The Author

V ivienne Wei set foot on the beautiful campus of Dartmouth College in Hanover, New Hampshire, leaving the bustling cosmopolitan Shanghai by herself at age eighteen. Since then, she has lived in London, Milan, Barcelona, New York, Boston and the San Francisco Bay Area. From Wall Street to Silicon Valley, she has always worked and excelled in a male-dominant environment.

Her previous experiences pale next to her transition to motherhood. Through research and interviews, Vivienne shares many surprises that women discover only after having children. After having had her second daughter, Vivienne outlines strategies for excelling in the transition to motherhood without derailing your career. She is a graduate of Harvard Business School and lives in the San Francisco Bay Area with her husband and two daughters.

Endnotes

1 "Gender Pay Inequality." The US Congress Joint Economic Committee." https://www.jec.senate.gov/public/_cache/files/0779dc2f-4a4e-4386-b847-9ae919735acc/gender-pay-inequality---us-congress-joint-economic-committee.pdf?linkId=34023341. Accessed 18 Jul. 2018.

2 "Americans with a college degree 1940 ...." https://www.statista.com/statistics/184272/educational-attainment-of-college-diploma-or-higher-by-gender/. Accessed 14 Jun. 2018.

3 "First Time Mothers at Work." https://www.dol.gov/wb/First-Time_Mothers_final_508.pdf. Accessed 14 Jun. 2018.

4 "First Time Mothers at Work." https://www.dol.gov/wb/First-Time_Mothers_final_508.pdf. Accessed 20 Jun. 2018.

5 "What to Expect When You're Expecting at Work." https://www.salesforce.com/blog/2018/03/what-to-expect-when-youre-expecting-at-work.html. Accessed 13 Jul. 2918.

6 "8 rights of pregnant women at work - CNN Money." 25 Jul. 2014, http://money.cnn.com/2014/07/25/news/economy/rights-pregnant-workers/index.html. Accessed 15 Jun. 2018.

7 "Maternity store giant to pay $375,000 to settle EEOC pregnancy discrimination and retaliation lawsuit." https://www.eeoc.gov/eeoc/newsroom/release/1-8-07.cfm. Accessed 13 July. 2018.

8 "Privilege in the Workplace: The Missing Element in Antidiscrimination Law by Stephanie M. Wildman - Santa Clara Law Digital Commons." https://digitalcommons.law.scu.edu/facpubs/442/. Accessed 3 Aug. 2018.

[9]   Joan C. Williams, Rachel Dempsey, "What Works for Women at Work". New York: New York University Press, 2014, 132. Accessed 31 Jul. 2018.

[10]   "When Is It Safe to Announce Your Pregnancy? - Healthline." 21 Jul. 2016, https://www.healthline.com/health/pregnancy/when-to-announce-your-pregnancy. Accessed 18 Jun. 2018.

[11]   "Higher Returns with Women in Decision-Making Positions - Credit ...." 3 Oct. 2016, https://www.credit-suisse.com/articles/news-and-expertise/2016/10/en/higher-returns-with-women-in-decision-making-positions.html. Accessed 15 Jun. 2018.

[12]   "The Right and Wrong Ways to Help Pregnant Workers." 27 Sep. 2016, https://hbr.org/2016/09/the-right-and-wrong-ways-to-help-pregnant-workers. Accessed 15 Jun. 2018.

[13]   "Working while pregnant is much more common than it used to be ...." 31 Mar. 2015, http://www.pewresearch.org/fact-tank/2015/03/31/working-while-pregnant-is-much-more-common-than-it-used-to-be/. Accessed 18 Jun. 2018.

[14]   "Why women leave tech: It's the culture, not because 'math is ... - Fortune." 2 Oct. 2014, http://fortune.com/2014/10/02/women-leave-tech-culture/. Accessed 15 Jun. 2018.

[15]   "The Use of Affinity Groups by Fortune 100 Firms - North American ...." http://www.na-businesspress.com/JBD/GlassmanAM_Web17_2_.pdf. Accessed 15 Jun. 2018.

[16]   "Women's Leadership Summit: Advancing Women in the ... - Salesforce." https://www.salesforce.com/video/183641/. Accessed 31 Jul. 2018.

[17] "Fast-Track Women and the "Choice" to Stay Home ... - SAGE Journals." http://journals.sagepub.com/doi/abs/10.1177/0002716204268552. Accessed 15 Jun. 2018.

[18] "Studies Show What Happens to Marriages After Having Kids | Fortune." 9 May. 2016, http://fortune.com/2016/05/09/mothers-marriage-parenthood/. Accessed 15 Jun. 2018.

[19] "Dads Expect Better - National Partnership for Women & Families." 1 Jun. 2012, http://go.nationalpartnership.org/site/DocServer/Dads_Expect_Better_June_2012.pdf. Accessed 15 Jun. 2018.

[20] "The Second Shift: Working Families and the Revolution at Home." https://books.google.com/books/about/The_Second_Shift.html?id=St_6kWcPJS8C. Accessed 13 Jul. 2018.

[21] "Women in the Workplace 2017." https://womenintheworkplace.com/. Accessed 15 Jun. 2018.

[22] "Employee Benefits Survey." Mar. 2017. https://www.bls.gov/ncs/ebs/benefits/2017/ownership/civilian/table32a.htm. Accessed 14 Jul. 2018.

[23] "Deloitte Survey: Less Than Half Of People Surveyed Feel Their Organization Helps Men Feel Comfortable Taking Parental Leave." https://www.prnewswire.com/news-releases/deloitte-survey-less-than-half-of-people-surveyed-feel-their-organization-helps-men-feel-comfortable-taking-parental-leave-300284822.html. Accessed 14 Jul. 2018.

[24] "Brain Connectivity Study Reveals Striking Differences ... - Penn Medicine." https://www.pennmedicine.org/news/news-releases/2013/december/brain-connectivity-study-revea. Accessed 15 Jun. 2018.

[25]   "In China, It's the Grandparents Who 'Lean In' - The Atlantic."
30 Sep. 2013, https://www.theatlantic.com/china/archive/2013/09/
in-china-its-the-grandparents-who-lean-in/280097/. Accessed
15 Jun. 2018.

[26]   "Interviews – Expecting at Work." http://expectingatwork.com/
interviews/. Accessed 3 Aug. 2018.

[27]   "Sleep Deprivation and New Parents - Consumer HealthDay."
https://consumer.healthday.com/encyclopedia/parenting-31/
parenting-health-news-525/sleep-deprivation-and-new-
parents-643886.html. Accessed 31 Jul. 2018.

[28]   "Sleep Deprivation 'Can Cost Companies Billions' and ... -
Newsweek." https://www.newsweek.com/sleep-deprivation-costs-
employers-rude-577132. Accessed 31 Jul. 2018.

[29]   "30-Day Trial: A Review of The Snoo – a $1200 Robotic ...
- Fathercraft." 4 Mar. 2018, https://fathercraft.com/30-day-trial-
review-snoo-1200-robotic-bassinet/. Accessed 1 Aug. 2018.

[30]   "These 10 countries have the best parental ...." 22 Aug. 2016,
http://www.businessinsider.com/countries-with-best-parental-
leave-2016-8. Accessed 19 Jun. 2018.

[31]   "10 things that make Sweden family-friendly - Sweden.se." 10 Jan.
2018, https://sweden.se/society/10-things-that-make-sweden-family-
friendly/. Accessed 19 Jun. 2018.

[32]   "There Are Significant Business Costs to Replacing Employees
...." 16 Nov. 2012, https://www.americanprogress.org/issues/
economy/reports/2012/11/16/44464/there-are-significant-business-
costs-to-replacing-employees/. Accessed 15 Jun. 2018.

[33]   "When Google increased paid maternity leave, the rate at
which new ...." 28 Jan. 2016, https://qz.com/604723/when-google-

increased-paid-maternity-leave-the-rate-at-which-new-mothers-quit-dropped-50/. Accessed 15 Jun. 2018.

34   Lacy, Sarah. *Uterus is a Feature, Not a Bug.* New York: Harper Collins, 2017. Print.

35   "U.S. Fertility Rate Fell to a Record Low, for a Second Straight Year ...." 16 May. 2018, https://www.nytimes.com/2018/05/17/us/fertility-rate-decline-united-states.html. Accessed 19 Jun. 2018.

36   "U.S. Parents Are Sweating And Hustling To Pay For Child Care : NPR." 22 Oct. 2016, https://www.npr.org/2016/10/22/498590650/u-s-parents-are-sweating-and-hustling-to-pay-for-child-care. Accessed 15 Jun. 2018.

37   "Child Care Regulations - California Department of Social Services." http://www.cdss.ca.gov/inforesources/Letters-Regulations/Legislation-and-Regulations/Community-Care-Licensing-Regulations/Child-Care. Accessed 31 Jul. 2018.

38   "This Nonprofit Wants To Put Stay-At-Home Moms Back To ... - Fortune." 22 Mar. 2016, http://fortune.com/2016/03/22/path-forward-returnship/. Accessed 15 Jun. 2018.

39   "Returnships for women won't fix the career break penalty." 21 Mar. 2017, http://theconversation.com/returnships-for-women-wont-fix-the-career-break-penalty-74472. Accessed 15 Jun. 2018.

40   "Don't Worry, Working Moms - The New York Times." 3 Aug. 2010, https://economix.blogs.nytimes.com/2010/08/03/dont-worry-working-moms/. Accessed 15 Jun. 2018.

41   "Kids Benefit From Having a Working Mom - HBS Working Knowledge." 15 May. 2015, https://hbswk.hbs.edu/item/kids-benefit-from-having-a-working-mom. Accessed 15 Jun. 2018.

[42] "Motivation to Manage: A Study of Women in Chinese ... - SAGE Journals." http://journals.sagepub.com/doi/abs/10.1177/0021886397332006. Accessed 15 Jun. 2018.

[43] "China GDP: how it has changed since 1980 | News | theguardian.com." 22 Mar. 2012, https://www.theguardian.com/news/datablog/2012/mar/23/china-gdp-since-1980. Accessed 15 Jun. 2018.

[44] "Gender discrimination comes in many forms for today's working women." 14 Dec. 2017, http://www.pewresearch.org/fact-tank/2017/12/14/gender-discrimination-comes-in-many-forms-for-todays-working-women/. Accessed 15 Jun. 2018.

[45] "Why women leave tech: It's the culture, not because 'math is ... - Fortune." 2 Oct. 2014, http://fortune.com/2014/10/02/women-leave-tech-culture/. Accessed 15 Jun. 2018.

[46] https://www.nytimes.com/2003/10/26/magazine/the-opt-out-revolution.html

[47] https://www.forbes.com/sites/kashmirhill/2012/05/24/sheryl-sandberg-to-harvard-biz-grads-find-a-rocket-ship/#cb42bd03b37a

[48] "The 50 Most Powerful Moms of 2017 | Working Mother." https://www.workingmother.com/50-most-powerful-moms-2017. Accessed 15 Jun. 2018.

[49] "Parenthood and Productivity of Highly Skilled Labor - Federal Reserve ...." 11 Jan. 2014, https://files.stlouisfed.org/files/htdocs/wp/2014/2014-001.pdf. Accessed 15 Jun. 2018.

[50] "Oxytocin hormone inhibits fear center in brain, shows ... - News Medical." 14 Nov. 2014, https://www.news-medical.net/news/20141114/Oxytocin-hormone-inhibits-fear-center-in-brain-shows-study.aspx.

[51] https://www.dol.gov/whd/regs/compliance/whdfs73.htm

[52] "Breastfeeding Rates | Breastfeeding | CDC." 1 Dec. 2017, https://www.cdc.gov/breastfeeding/data/nis_data/index.htm. Accessed 15 Jun. 2018.

[53] "Why relationships are so important for children and young people ...." https://www.mentalhealth.org.uk/blog/why-relationships-are-so-important-children-and-young-people. Accessed 15 Jun. 2018.

[54] "Emily Chang - LeanIn.org." https://leanin.org/stories/emily-chang. Accessed 15 Jun. 2018.

[55] "Making time for kids? Study says quality trumps quantity. - The ...." 28 Mar. 2015, https://www.washingtonpost.com/local/making-time-for-kids-study-says-quality-trumps-quantity/2015/03/28/10813192-d378-11e4-8fce-3941fc548f1c_story.html. Accessed 15 Jun. 2018.

Made in the USA
Middletown, DE
25 January 2019